GAME PLAN

Develop a
Spiritually Winning Strategy
for Adults and Teens
in Today's Culture

Joe Wells, M.Min.

KAIO PUBLICATIONS, INC.

Copyright © 2019 Joe Wells and Kaio Publications, Inc. All rights reserved.

No part of this book may be used or reproduced in any manner whatsoever without written permission of the author and publisher.

All scripture notations are from the New American Standard Bible®, Copyright © 1960, 1962, 1963, 1968, 1971, 1972, 1973, 1975, 1977, 1995 The Lockman Foundation, Publishers, unless otherwise noted.

For more information contact Kaio Publications, Inc. at:
223 Town Center Parkway, #118, Spring Hill, TN 37174

To order additional copies of *Game Plan* visit www.kaiopublications.org.

Book edited by Gina Rose • Book design by D.J. Smith

Cover background and interior images by ThinkStock

ISBN 978-1-7326661-2-2

Library of Congress Control Number: 2011933527

FIRST EDITION

Printed in the United States of America

To my wife, Erin, and our children – Colton, Michala, Camden, and Bennett. Thank you for your unending love, support, and laughter. You are the faces I see first when I think of *Game Plan*. Always remember our number one goal – Heaven.

To my parents, Wayne and Cindy – thank you for loving Jesus and each other. Your teaching continues today.

Visit the official *Game Plan* website for the most current cultural headlines impacting your family.

www.familygameplan.org

CONTENTS

PREFACE IX

INTRODUCTION X

CHAPTER 1 WHO ARE THEY? 1

CHAPTER 2 MARKETING TO TEENS 11

CHAPTER 3 THE CRACK IN THE FOUNDATION 25

CHAPTER 4 WHAT DID WE REALLY THINK WOULD HAPPEN? 51

CHAPTER 5 AGENDAS ATTACKING AMERICA PART 1 71

CHAPTER 6 AGENDAS ATTACKING AMERICA PART 2 91

CHAPTER 7 WE MUST GET BACK TO 111

CHAPTER 8 THE ATTACK WE'RE UNDER 133

CHAPTER 9 THE SEXUALIZATION OF AMERICA 159

CHAPTER 10 RAISE THE BAR 179

PRACTICE DRILLS 197

ENDNOTES 217

APPENDIX 229

COACH'S NOTES 237

PREFACE

In 1997, while still a teen myself, I began working with a small congregation in Godly, Texas, as a Bible class teacher for the teens. I've always seen the value in reaching young people with the Gospel of Jesus Christ; however, the more years I've experienced in local ministry working with teens and families, the more I've learned. The Gospel is still the power of God for salvation, just as Paul wrote in Romans 1:16; however, in today's culture, there is so much "noise" that it makes it difficult for most teenagers to hear that message. While in times past, it possibly could have been assumed that the majority of young people believed the Bible to be inspired by God and the source of truth - that simply isn't the case anymore. In our politically correct society, our young people are taught to drift in the middle ground – drowning in the deep of unbiblical tolerance. It's this clash between Biblical authority and humanistic logic that traps many of our youth and renders them motionless and worse yet – apathetic.

Game Plan was born in reflection of this epidemic. Something has to be done to help teens combat the "noise" so they can hear better the Gospel. As I look in the Bible, parents hold the single most important role in this task; however, many parents are simply either ill-equipped or so busy with their own lives that they aren't as proactive as they need to be. This doesn't mean they're not loving parents, but it does show how we can focus so much on providing a roof over their head, food on the table, and clothes on their back but miss the most important aspect of being a parent or adult leader – their spiritual well-being.

I pray this book will encourage you to not only be informed about the culture our teens are surrounded by, but it will inspire you and equip you to help them. The teenagers in your life need you to be proactive. Help them understand the winning *Game Plan* and always keep in the front of their minds the ultimate goal: Heaven.

Because of HIM,
Joe Wells

INTRODUCTION

The stage is set, and what a stage it is! Your teen will face the biggest and the most advanced opponent of their short life. Sure, this child has had a few victories; however, you, as the adult, know that he's not ready for this challenge. The opponent is stronger and better equipped. His scheme, his plan of attack, has caused countless numbers of individuals to crumble and collapse in shameful defeat. You're not a prophet, but if there were ever any signs of a pending defeat – this scenario has them all over it. In your mind, you envision the worst outcome possible – your precious child, the one whom you've seen grow from a small innocent baby into the individual before you today, lying dead on the battlefield.

If you could help this teen, what would you do? What would you say? Would you downplay the strength of the opponent or would you expose it so as to warn against overlooking the obvious? Would you study the enemy's plan of attack and his methods? Would you train the teen to be able to recognize what the enemy might do on the field, or would you simply let him learn by trial and error? If you could equip them to not only survive but win – would you? It might mean they wouldn't like you at times. It possibly could cost you a "friendship" with them – at least as defined by the world. Would you be willing to get engaged and help?

While the above scenario might sound fictitious, sadly it's all too real. The Bible explains that the devil is like a roaring lion. He's prowling around seeking to devour those who are unaware and stand alone on his battlefield. While we would love to think that Satan is only going to come after the "grown-ups" – the supposedly spiritually stronger ones, doesn't it make more sense that he would be more interested in hunting those who are least experienced, typically the weakest spiritually – i.e. young people? As their beliefs about everything from family roles to politics to matters of doctrine are continually being fashioned, their receptive minds stand as both a great positive and a fearful negative. Positive in the sense that as parents, elders, deacons, Bible class teachers, and ministers you stand as an important influence in their life to guide them in the Truth of God's Word. Yet negative for a very similar reason – they are open to be influenced by the darkness of this world.

Did God intend for young people to navigate this vast ocean on their own? Was it His plan all along that they would be abandoned to fend for themselves, or did He give instructions to parents, and at times elders, teachers, evangelists, to engage in the spiritual training of the young? The answer is very clear as His intent all along was for adults – especially parents – to be the coaches that would prepare the children as they grew to be true disciples of God – following the teaching revealed in His Word. It is up to these coaches to know the enemy's attacks and to be able to equip the young to draw near to God.

If this is going to happen, and the worst possible outcome of the battle be avoided, adults must understand the times teenagers are growing up in – the thought processes, the messages, the influences, and the lowered expectations. I'm not suggesting simply knowing these elements so as to be able to complain about them over a cup of coffee, but rather to be informed as to what teenagers are facing, and more importantly so you can help them combat the anti-Biblical message and grow closer and closer to God in full obedience to Him. You must spend time preparing yourself so that you are not simply reacting to situations. You will never respond in the best manner if you simply react which is why I encourage you – the parents – the elders – the deacons – the Bible class teachers – the ministers – to be proactive in helping the teens in your life. Spend time now developing a *Game Plan* that is according to God's Word. Walk with your teens as they grow, understanding they've yet to reach full maturity; therefore, they need you to serve as a guide and a mentor to them. Don't be afraid to make the hard decisions. To be the coach is not for the weak; however, someone has to wear the whistle. If you don't, this world will. Don't let that happen. Develop a *Game Plan*!

PHYSICALLY, THEY COME FROM GOD; HOWEVER, AS MODERN TEENAGERS, OUR SOCIETY HAS CREATED THEM.

CHAPTER 1

WHO ARE THEY?

In America alone, there are roughly 43.5 million of them.[1] On a quick trip to the mall, you'll be surrounded by them. Visiting a burger joint, you'll see them in small packs. A few might even be spotted hovering by a street corner in your neighborhood. It's quite possible you've passed them while driving, or been served by one at the local ice cream shop.

You notice they usually look a little different. The way they dress might shock you. You see the loose, baggy pants on some with shorts hanging out of the back waistband. Others wear pants so tight you know they can't breathe well. You wonder how they put that color in their hair, or better yet, why they would want that color in their hair in the first place. You see the nose piercing along with the lip piercings on some, and hear, at times, what seems to be a new and foreign language. You simply look the other way while thinking, "If I don't make eye contact with them, they'll leave me alone."

What strange creature is this, you ask? If you said an alien with a strange choice in dress, a hunger for burgers, and a desire to pierce its body in the strangest of places, then you are… not correct. However, if you said, "What is an American teenager?" then prepare to hear *Jeopardy* host Alex Trebek applaud you for your correct answer.

Next, you might ask where this strange breed of being comes from. In Genesis chapter 1, we read of man and woman being created in the image

of God (v. 27). However, it's the very next verse (v. 28) that brings us face-to-face with the reality that teenagers come from God. Man and woman were told to be fruitful and multiply– to bring children into the world. It is God's design for those children to grow in age and also in maturity, which means the teenager was God's idea, and they are considered a blessing (Psalm 127:3).

However, while the Bible is very clear on where teens physically come from, this doesn't give us a lot of insight into how America has yielded the teenagers we see today. How did we arrive at this place in history, with these strange creatures we call teenagers?

DEFINING A CHILD

You might not be aware of this, but the word "teenager" was not found in American vocabulary much before 1941. It actually was derived from the noun "teenage". While there were other names used to describe individuals going through the teen years such as "teener" (American English 1894) and "teen" (documented as early as 1818), the strength of these words were nothing in comparison with how this demographic was described in and around 1941. There was a reason another word came about and a reason why the name "teenager" became very significant in our culture.[2]

> **By Def·i·ni·tion**
>
> **teen·age·er** —n
> a person between the ages of 13 and 19 inclusive

Before the late 1930s and early 1940s, the age divisions in America were pretty simple. You were either considered to be an adolescent, an adult, or a person of old age. These groups were not generally distinguished by a person's actual years lived, but by his or her capacity to handle responsibilities. Thus it was not uncommon to have situations such as a 17-year-old George Washington being employed as the first surveyor of Culpepper County, Virginia, and tasked with creating the layout for the county courthouse.[3] It was understood and accepted that those who were adolescents should aspire to reach adulthood and for those who were adults to work as hard as their bodies would allow before they reached the last division, old age.

In the 1930s, the limited job front of the Great Depression was pushing many teenagers out of the work place. The Fair Standards Labor Act of 1938, limiting the number of hours a "child" could work and requiring a "fair" wage be paid to all laborers, finalized a shift in hiring practices. With fewer employers hiring younger employees, this group now officially classified as children was left with a dilemma: fewer full-time jobs + more time = "what am I going to do?". The answer many teenagers turned to was school; in 1940, for the first time in history, the majority of 17-year-olds earned a high school diploma.[4] With this major shift of youth out of the workplace and into school, combined with the conclusion of World War 2 and a tremendous increase in the number of children in the United States (76 million),[5] the modern teenager was born.

A NEW GENERATION

Today's generation of teens is referred to as "the Millennials." As with each generation, this one is unique; however, the problems they face are very similar to that of "Generation X" (born 1965-1980). The pressures of family, society, school, and various physiological changes make being a teenager not only difficult, but confusing at times. With the increase in technology (cell phones, Internet, etc.) and the rapid movement of the family structure away from a normative model (i.e. the ideal, what "ought to be") and toward sociological reality (i.e. what current reality is), we are seeing a generation that thinks and acts very differently from those that preceded it. Objective truth has given way to relativism. Their concept of dating, sex, and marriage is shaped by an increase in cohabitation amongst adults. Moral dilemmas such as euthanasia, abortion, homosexuality, and AIDS remain and continue to grow as problematic issues. Understanding this demographic and their culture is crucial in reaching them with the wonderful message of Jesus Christ. For our teaching and methods to be relevant, we must understand not only the physical and emotional changes which normally take place, but the influences surrounding these young people.

Adolescence can be considered the second revolution in a person's developmental process; between the ages of 10 and 20 a new person blossoms through physical, emotional, social, moral, and intellectual changes.[6] This process, commonly referred to as puberty, begins around the age of 12 for girls and age 14 for boys, although it can begin much earlier. As hormones change, as the inevitable acne sets in, and as boys' voices change and girls' menstrual cycles begin, adolescents tend to bounce between emotional highs and lows. They may experience interest in areas they had previously avoided (i.e. relationships with the opposite sex, drugs, or alcohol), and with increased social pressures, they are at an increased risk of developing disorders such as anorexia nervosa and bulimia.[7]

All of these changes can result in what psychologist Erik Erikson described as an identity crisis. Their thoughts are consumed with questions such as, "who am I?", "do I belong?" and "where am I going?" These questions may be reflected in relationships with parents and peers as well as in the way they dress, act, and talk. Psychologist David Elkind described teenagers' behavior in these areas as a performance to imaginary audiences.[8] Because teens tend to think they are always being watched and criticized, embarrassment comes easily, and they may be influenced to dress and behave in certain ways.

Within the highly vulnerable situation surrounding teenagers, there are two major influencers in their lives helping shaping them. The first is family influence. According to the National Marriage Project, the divorce rate in America has doubled since 1960, hitting an all-time high in 1980 and currently hovering at approximately 41-45 percent.[9] While this statistic is not as high as it has been in previous years, we should not celebrate it. Many who study the family have discovered that while divorce

WHO ARE THEY?

Erickson's Stage Theory in its Final Version[10]

Age	Conflict	Resolution or "Virtue"	Culmination In Old Age
Infancy (0-1 Year)	Basic Trust vs. Mistrust	Hope	Appreciation of interdependence and relatedness
Early Childhood (1-3 years)	Autonomy vs. Shame	Will	Acceptance of the cycle of life, from integration to disintegration
Play age (3-6 years)	Initiative vs. Guilt	Purpose	Humor; empathy; resilience
School Age (6-12 years)	Industry vs. Inferiority	Competence	Humility; acceptance of the course of one's life and unfulfilled hopes
Adolescence (12-19 years)	Identity vs. Confusion	Fidelity	Sense of complexity of life; merging of sensory, logical and loving freely
Early Adulthood (20-25 years)	Intimacy vs. Isolation	Love	Sense of complexity of relationships; value tenderness and loving freely
Adulthood (26-64 Years)	Generativity vs. Stagnation	Care	Caritas, caring for others, and agape, empathy and concern
Old Age (65-Death)	Integrity vs. Despair	Wisdom	Existential identity; a sense of integrity strong enough to withstand physical disintegration

is decreasing, the rate of cohabitation is on the rise. Today, roughly 40 percent of all births are to unmarried women.[11]

Alongside the crumbling of the family structure in many American homes today, overspending and borrowing has led to the problem of overworked parents. According to The Plastic Safety Net, research show that credit card debt in America has almost tripled since 1989 and increased 31 percent since 2000. Americans now owe an estimated $900 billion in credit card debt with the average low and middle-income families owing $9,827.[12] These factors have resulted in overstressed and overworked parents who struggle to find the time to raise their children.

In 1975, 39 percent of mothers with children under the age of 6 worked outside of the home. By 1990, that number had risen to above 50 percent; the most recent statistics is 64 percent.[13] Along with this, we are seeing an increase in the hours that fathers of school age children are working. According to the National Sleep Foundation, the 40-hour work week is quickly becoming a thing of the past, being replaced by 50- and even 60-hour work weeks. The end result is an increased amount of fatigue, poorer job performances, and an increase in the stress level of the parent.

The collateral damage can be seen in the decreased amount of time that many parents spend with their children. The debate of quality time versus quantity time is simply an excuse to dismiss the stark reality that our children are oftentimes left to fend for themselves. Teens today may wish their parents had more time for them; however, the dark reality is that more debt means parents must work more hours to pay the bills. Subsequently, time with their children suffers, while parents convince themselves it won't have that much of an effect on the children.

However, when teenagers are left to raise themselves, they will turn to the second of the biggest influences in their life: current culture. This includes media, with the values and morals seen on television and heard through current music.

Rolling Stones Magazine conducted a survey in the early 1990s in which

WHO ARE THEY?

they asked their readers to vote on their favorite songs of all time. The results of their studies introduced the world to individuals like Cathy, a 16-year-old from California who had grown up in an abusive household. In her essay, defending her choice of favorite songs of all time, she wrote, "I had been an abused child all my life, and something about the music moved me. Feelings of hurt and anger that had been bottled up all those years took over. I started shaking and crying, and that night I made the decision that what they were doing to me was wrong and I wasn't going to let anyone use me as a punching bag ever again." [14] Cathy went on to describe her battle through the courts and how she ended up moving in with her grandparents. However, it was her connection with her favorite song that she would credit for keeping her from committing suicide in the midst of some very dark hours in her life.

Teenagers find it very easy to make a connection with music when artists portray emotions teens understand. Songs with messages about hurt, pain, suicide, violence, drug dealings, and sex are thrown together with happiness, love, joy, and fulfillment in the great mixing bowl called music.

Robert Pittman, founder and chairman of MTV, said, "The strongest appeal you can make...is emotionally. If you can get their emotions going, [make them] forget their logic, you've got' em." [15] He's right! Teenagers are often driven by their emotions. One day they're up and the next day they're down. The problem is that the music industry knows this, and uses it to target adolescents and teens. Their goal is not to entertain, but rather, as Pittman puts it, to "own" their audience. They want to bring the teens into their world, where they drive the train. They want to impress their values and morals on young people to create a generation of followers who will adopt their views and their lifestyles.

Marilyn Manson is quoted as saying, "Every culture is reflected by its artists." [16] This is sadly demonstrated in a recent interview with teen idol Justin Bieber who, when asked if a person should wait until they were married before engaging in sex said, "I think you should just wait for the person you're in love with." In the same interview, when asked about homosexuality being a sin Bieber replied, "It's everyone's own decision to do that... it doesn't affect me and shouldn't affect anyone else."[17] Despite coming from a Christian background and being taught the words of the Bible, his answers to these simple questions demonstrate all too well how an artist can reflect current culture and the post-modern belief system.

However, a quick look into the career of an artist such as Madonna and one can see that Manson's statement is only partially true. In the mid-1980s, Madonna came on the scene with a blast. She was radically different and immediately made a connection with preteens and young teenagers. She went beyond pushing the envelope in the area of sexuality both in the way she dressed and in her songs (i.e. "Like a Virgin"). As she continued to grow in popularity she became a cultural icon that teens looked up to and wanted to become. Teens dressed like her, wore their hair like she did, and even changed the way they talked- a perfect example of a culture following the artist.

Over the years, Madonna has continued to evolve her image in order to keep up with the times and has been able to endure the changing climate in the music world. But while her music might have changed, her basic message of pushing immorality has not. This was evident in the 2003 MTV Video Music Awards, when she and Britney Spears exchanged an open-mouth kiss in front of millions of people. This was presented as a "passing of the torch" moment as Spears and Christina Aguilera, both former Disney's Mickey Mouse Clubhouse kids, came out dressed in white, wedding attire, and Madonna was dressed in black, groom attire. A sign of the times, indeed!

So, where did "they" come from? Physically, they come from God; however, as modern teenagers, our society has created them. We created them as we removed them from the workplace and put them in an environment where they spend more time around their peers than they do adults. We created them when we developed the marketing campaigns that

WHO ARE THEY?

bombarded them in the late 1930s, 1940s, and 1950s, in order to capture a group of new customers which had not firmly existed before. We created them in the sense that we allowed philosophies and theories to dictate the process a child is to go through, including the acceptance that teenage rebellion is completely "natural."

WHAT AT FIRST HAD SEEMED LIKE A USELESS DEMOGRAPHIC FOR RETAILERS TO PURSUE QUICKLY MORPHED INTO A CAPTIVE, BRAND NEW MARKET THAT RETAILERS EXCITEDLY CHASED IN ORDER TO EXPAND THEIR CUSTOMER BASE.

CHAPTER 2

MARKETING TO TEENS:
HOW A FOCUSED EFFORT HELPED SHAPE AMERICA

Imagine walking into your old high school. You remember the familiar old brick look as you approach the front of the building. The big metal door still has that same old squeaky noise, but your walk down memory lane comes to a screeching halt as you must pass through metal detectors to gain entry into the hallways. You notice the office is in the same place, but it's been redesigned. The classroom doors open to the same space you remember; however, upon looking in, you realize that you're not in Kansas anymore, and the high-tech tornado has crashed right into the classrooms.

These changes are striking, but then your jaw drops as you notice another change: billboards are plastered across the lockers. Advertisements selling electronics, books, video games, and multiple food options fly right before your face. They swirl around your head until finally you can't take it anymore – you have to walk on. You enter the cafeteria and realize that it's no escape from the Twilight Zone; you've only entered a deeper phase. You knew you would see posters teaching kids about healthy eating, but you never expected a fast food chain to be the group sponsoring the posters. You take quick strides to the library, thinking it will be a safe place, free from the marketing serpent, but as you spot the clown dressed in

GAME PLAN

yellow with the red hair teaching a group of kids, you quickly realize that advertisement brainwashing has permeated every place in your old school.

Why would these companies invest so much money to advertise to our kids? What would they possibly stand to gain from placing ads in an environment where the majority of the people who would see them are under the age of 18? Maybe they know something we don't.

Are you aware...

- Companies spend on average roughly $17 billion each year to market to teenagers? That is a 170 percent increase just since 1983.[1]

- Children under the age of 14 will spend roughly $40 billion each year?[2]

- It's estimated that teenage spending will total $208.7 billion in 2011?[3]

- Estimates show that children ages 12 to 14 years have an average annual income of $2,167?[4]

- Teens 15 to 17-years-old have an estimated annual income of $4,023?[5]

It appears these marketing companies spend so much money each year trying to attract underage buyers because there is a huge amount of money to be made! Okay-"money talks" – but when did this craze of attracting teenagers as a customer base really begin to make an impact on our culture? To answer this question, we must venture back in America to the end of World War 2.

As young men returned home from foreign shores, the American economy saw a huge boost. Between 1939 and 1950, managerial incomes rose 45 percent. Supervisors' salaries climbed 83 percent, and production workers' earnings shot up 106 percent. With such increases in income, more American families could afford middle-class comforts. The number of car registrations grew to 40 million by 1950, an increase of 14 million from just five years earlier. The number of single-housing starts grew from

114,000 in 1944 to nearly 1.7 million in 1950. While the war had taught teens the valuable lesson of sacrifice, it also stirred their desire for material goods such as records, clothes, cars – items that were rapidly becoming seen as a standard part of teenage life.[6]

While most in the 1940s marketing world didn't believe the teenage demographic was something to waste time on, 51-year-old grandmother Helen Valentine saw potential. In 1944, Valentine launched *Seventeen* magazine and began her crusade to convince retailers and manufacturers to target teenage girls.[7] Her campaign was vindicated when the very first edition of *Seventeen* sold out 400,000 copies within two days and the second printing of the first issue sold 500,000 in the same time frame. Within 16 months, the magazine circulation topped 1 million subscribers, and no one could deny the success of Valentine's concept.[8]

With this base, *Seventeen* decided to reach out to retailers, to yield additional income through advertising. To accomplish this task, professional research team Benson and Benson, of Princeton, New Jersey, created "Teena", a fictional girl with money of her own to purchase any interesting product she saw advertised in *Seventeen* magazine. As the readers were asked to take the survey on behalf of Teena, the researchers were able to feel the pulse of their market, and what they found rattled the cage of that marketing serpent:

- 66 percent of those who took the survey expected to be homemakers.
- 77 percent already influenced their parents' purchasing decisions on items such as groceries, furniture, radios and phonographs.
- 65 percent had a strong interest in clothes.
- 87 percent influenced their friends when it came to selecting clothes.[9]

GAME PLAN

The retailers began to comprehend that if they could sell just a few teenage girls on their products, then word-of-mouth marketing would ultimately sell to their friends as well.

It didn't take very long before clothing manufacturers jumped onboard to work with *Seventeen,* not only selling their products in the publication, but also designing clothing specifically for the magazine's readers. By the early 1950s, cosmetic companies Ponds and Woodbury jumped in with their brands of teenage makeup. Soon grocery chains such as A&P and Grand Union and food manufacturer Pillsbury were buying advertising space as well. What at first had seemed like a useless demographic for retailers to pursue quickly morphed into a captive, brand new market that retailers excitedly chased in order to expand their customer base.

In 1961, *Seventeen* celebrated its 17th birthday and gave its readers a general idea of where it had been and where it was going:

> "When Seventeen was born in 1944, we made one birthday wish: that this magazine would give stature to the teen-age years, give teen-agers a sense of identity, of purpose, of belonging. In what kind of world did we make our wish? A world in which teen-agers were the forgotten, the ignored generation. In stores, teen-agers shopped for clothes in adults' or children's departments, settling for fashions too old or too young... They suffered the hundred pains and uncertainties of adolescence in silence...In 1961, as we blow out the candles on our seventeenth birthday cake, the accent everywhere is on youth. The needs, the wants, even the whims of teen-agers are catered to by almost every major industry. But what is more important, teens themselves have found a sense of direction in a very difficult world...Around the entire world, they are exerting powerful moral and political pressures. When a girl celebrates her thirteenth birthday today, she knows who she is. She's a teen-ager – and proud of it."[10]

MARKETING TO TEENS

Now do you understand why the marketing serpent has attacked your school? It was purposed to happen as our society created the teenage demographic as a legitimate consumer base. So catch your breath. It's not going to go back to the way it was- and the serpent will continue to grow and look for other demographics to sink its teeth into next.

ROCK 'N' ROLL PROPELLED THE TEENAGER

Rock and Roll, in all its forms, gives us a microphone to communicate with the world. It has the power to bring nationalities and generations together, to elect world leaders, and to move people. No other art form has the social significance of Rock and Roll. You simply cannot understand Western Culture without taking a serious look at this music.[11]

This quote is from the Rock and Roll Hall of Fame and Museum in Cleveland, Ohio, a facility established to capture in one place the people and events that have contributed to this genre of music. The 150,000 square-foot museum stands seven stories tall, with a total of five theatres used for programs and concerts. Thousands of items of musical and cultural significance are on display, dated from the late 1800s to today. However, as the above statement claims, rock and roll is more than simply the music. It represents a transformation in American society as rhythm and blues melded with folk music, gospel hymns, blues, country, and bluegrass to ignite a fire throughout the younger generation. Individuals such as Benny Goodman, nicknamed "The King of Swing", brought bobby soxers to their feet with his big band swing music of the 20s and 30s; however, the craze of rock and roll overshadowed anything and everything America had seen before.

With America deeply segregated over race, the early pioneers of rock and roll didn't always get their due. Individuals such as Duke Ellington and Lionel Hampton, black musicians who played jazz music, were just

as talented as some of their white counterparts such as Glenn Miller; however, America was not ready to accept black musicians on equal

Duke Ellington

grounds, nor strong, pulsing rhythms designed to stir a dancing crowd. Songs such as "Don't Want No Skinny Woman," "Gotta Give Me What-cha Got," and "I Want a Bowlegged Woman" made it very clear that this type of music contained a highly sexual message, and was not appropriate for playing on the family radio- at least not when parents were around to listen.

Even with adults pushing against it, "race music" as some called it, began to pick up popularity as more and more radio stations began devoting programming time to it, often times at late hours of the night. Disc jockeys became a powerful influence, as teen audiences formed attachments to their favorite on-air personality, generating a loyalty and a following that would set the scene for the rock and roll explosion. Following Helen Valentine's school of thought, early 50s radio stations began to acknowledge the economic potential of the teenage market and offered the music teens wanted- not necessarily what their parents wanted for them.

In 1951, out of Cleveland, Ohio, a radio disc jockey named Alan Freed launched the "Moondog Show" on WJW radio. The show was designed to attract teenagers from all walks of life and from every race, capitalizing on the huge market. While there were beautiful songs atop the charts, songs like the Weavers' "Good Night Irene" (1950) and "Tennessee Waltz" (1951) by Patti Page, none brought on a dancing stir like what took place in "the Moondog House", a nickname for Freed's show. As the music played, and with the microphone turned on, Freed would drum along on a telephone book and shout with the music, encouraging teen listeners to dance along. [12]

MARKETING TO TEENS

With his popularity and following growing amongst teenagers from all racial backgrounds, Freed launched into the area of hosting live concerts. His most notable event was held on March 21, 1952, creatively coined "The Moondog Coronation Ball". With various popular artists set to perform, a crowd of over 9,000, most of them teenagers, poured into the Cleveland Arena for a night of music and dancing. With Alan Freed as the emcee, the show was kicked-off- and very soon afterwards was shut-down. While those inside were enjoying the music, twice as many outside the arena didn't want to be left out, so they stormed the gates and crashed the concert. While Freed would take the negative publicity on the chin and was even threatened with being arrested for inciting the crowd to act in ways that were illegal, *Billboard* and *Cashbox* magazines covered the story, generating national publicity for Freed and this brand of "rock 'n' roll", a term he started using to describe the music he was promoting.[13]

Moondog Coronation Ball Poster

This newfound publicity led rock 'n' roll records to sell like hotcakes amongst teenagers. In 1955 alone, teenagers reportedly accounted for 80 percent of rock 'n' roll sales; however parents and society as a whole were not as "on board". *Variety* magazine captured the concerns of the day when they printed, "Swing never had the moral threat of rock 'n' roll which is founded on an unabashed pitch for sex. Every note and vocal nuance is aimed in that direction." [14] It was obvious, if rock 'n' roll was ever going to catch on with adults in main stream America, it was going to have to change its image.

In 1955, Bill Haley and the Comets released "Rock Around the Clock", trying to clean up the lyrics and the reputation that rock 'n' roll was developing. The song became a nationwide hit after being featured in the movie *The Blackboard Jungle*, and Haley and his band became a national force to advance the genre. "We steer completely clear of anything suggestive," Haley is quoted as saying. "We take a lot of care with lyrics because we don't want to offend anybody."[15]

While Bill Haley and the Comets recognized the need to change the image of rock 'n' roll, their song's popularity was driven by its presence in a movie focused on teenage rebellion and high school violence; this fact only added to anti-rock sentiments. It was going to take more than one group to bring this brand of music into mainstream American acceptance. The quest to find the right performer with the right singing voice and style began… Enter the "King of Rock 'n' Roll".

Born in 1935 to a lower income family in Tupelo, Mississippi, Elvis Presley taught himself how to play the guitar. He would frequent gospel singings, soaking in the styles and abilities of spiritual singers. At the same time, he was listening on the radio to various blues artists such as Big Bill Broonzy and Arthur Crudup, despite his parents' disapproval. In 1955, with his good looks, unique clothing style, pomade in his jet black hair, and slick side burns, Elvis entered into a contract with RCA Victor that would forever change his life, the scene of rock 'n' roll, and the teenagers who would flock to see "The Pelvis" perform- a name given to him because of the provocative movements Elvis would make while performing. "He isn't afraid to express himself," one 15-year-old girl said. "When he does that…I get down on the floor and scream."[16] Even with this seemingly appropriate fit for the time and the music, Elvis was labeled a rebellious individual for the way he dressed and moved, and for the music he would sing.

In 1956, when Ed Sullivan signed Elvis to perform on his hit-making show "Toast of the Town", the young singer knew this was his opportunity to break into the mainstream. Toning down his look and pelvic gyrations, Elvis delivered a performance that led Sullivan to proclaim him a "real decent fine boy". With this referral, both Elvis and rock 'n' roll were

MARKETING TO TEENS

propelled into the popular market overnight. [17] Aided by Dick Clark's *American Bandstand*, with its wholesome image of teenage life, what was once considered rebellious teenage music quickly became a mass money-making machine that forever changed the teenage culture.

So what does the Rock and Roll Hall of Fame and Museum represent? Is their claim that *"no other art form has the social significance of Rock and Roll. You simply cannot understand Western Culture without taking a serious look at this music."* Is this true? Absolutely! The current state of America, and especially the teenage culture in America, is a direct result of events that played out in the 40s, 50s, and 60s. Rock 'n' roll played a significant part in both the breaking down of racial segregation and in the development of the modern day teenager.

SHAPED BY THE BIG SCREEN

"We, in the United States, are fortunate to have a school system that is a tribute to our communities and to our faith in American youth. Today we are concerned with juvenile delinquency-its causes-and its effects. We are especially concerned when this delinquency boils over into our schools. The scenes and incidents depicted here are fictional. However, we believe that public awareness is a first step toward a remedy for any problem. It is in this spirit and with this faith that 'Blackboard Jungle' was produced."[18]

Metro-Goldwyn-Mayer Corp.'s 1955 release of the movie *Blackboard Jungle* was a pivotal move in a society primed for the rise of the American teenager. With the conclusion of World War 2 and the increase amount of attention paid to the teenage demographic in the area of marketing and music, Hollywood was bound to turn their attention to this financially lucrative group; however, how would they connect with this group and what would keep teenagers coming back, movie after movie? The answer Hollywood gave and continues to give today is very simple: make movies that reflect the events of everyday teenage life. That's exactly why you read the above quotation in the opening portion of *Blackboard Jungle*, a movie about a teacher's attempt to connect with an out-of-control group of teenagers and the school environment that serves as their playground.

With the FBI stating that juvenile delinquency rose 45 percent between 1945 and 1953 and 55 percent between 1952 and 1957, teenage rebellion became a hot-button topic.[19] Both parents and government entities expressed concern that Hollywood was "glamorizing" the teenage rebel in movies like *The Wild One*, starring a young Marlon Brando as the leader of a motorcycle gang. Society worried that teenagers seeing the "nobody wants to mess with me" attitude and "the bad guys get the girls" motifs would begin to imitate what they saw on the big screen; the fear truly was that more teenage rebels would be produced.

Hollywood's answer remained simple. They refused to take credit for the increase in juvenile delinquency, simply claiming they were bringing something to the lime-light that was already taking place in America. To their credit, they were partially correct. With the final push of teenagers out of the workplace and into schools, the increase in teens' financial means, and the burst of music designed specifically to attract teenage customers, there was already a change in play when Hollywood began to produce what might be called "teenage-movies". However, to say they had nothing to do with developing teenage attitudes and expectations is a farce.

In 1955, Warner Bros. Pictures released what would become a culturally iconic movie entitled *Rebel Without a Cause*, starring James Dean and Natalie Wood. In keeping with concerns over juvenile delinquency, the character Dean played was a troubled teen whose family was forced to continually pick up and move in order to "deal" with his behavioral problems. Natalie Wood's character was, in contrast, a "good-girl" who sought to help Dean and ended up falling in love with the "bad-boy". While this seems to be an innocent enough storyline, further insight into the two characters brings to light the teenage rebellion involved.

James Dean

Both characters belong to families struggling to understand their teen, creating- or, as Hollywood would say, *demonstrating*- a "parents vs. teens" predicament. Jim Stark (Dean's character) has an overbearing mother and a father who lacks backbone. Even though Jim's father tries to stand up for him, his mother always wins in their arguments, causing Jim to question his father as a man. Natalie Wood's character, Judy, is a young teenage girl whose father doesn't know how to show her the proper affection. In her failed attempts to gain that from him, she is forced to look for it in another male- ultimately, in Jim.

With the release of this movie, the stage was set for a "parents vs. teens" or even "adults vs. teens" theme. Over the next few years, Hollywood would ride the wave, releasing movie after movie that demonstrated, and often rested solely on, this central theme. Movies such as *I Was a Teenage Werewolf* (1957), *I Was a Teenage Frankenstein* (1957), and *Invasion of the Saucer Men* (1957) all portrayed teenage protagonists who simply wanted to help or were trying to stand up against the antagonists- who often times took the form of teachers, parents, or other authority figures.

The early 1960s introduced the beach party movies of Frankie and Annette. A sense of nostalgia swept the country, as people sought to regain the innocence of the pre-World War 2 era. Meshing the innocence with the newly distinguished teenage culture, Hollywood presented movies such as *Ride the Wild Surf* (1964), *Beach Ball* (1965), and *Wild on the Beach* (1965) that showcased teenagers simply wanting to have fun and be carefree with their love interest. However, this return to innocence didn't last very long.

As the 1960s progressed, so did the outspokenness of the new Baby Boomers. The teenage culture continued to evolve into a new questioning of authority and speaking out against seeming injustice. As the Civil Rights movement progressed, and with the Vietnam War moving forward, teenagers deepened their counter-cultural, anti-authoritarian way of thinking, and Hollywood was right there to encourage them in what they sought. Movies such as *The Love-Ins* (1967), *Riot on Sunset Beach* (1967), and *Wild on the Streets* (1968) served as markers and rallying cries for standing up and being heard.

The 1970s brought epic films such as *Star Wars* (1977), *Jaws* (1975), and *Grease* (1978), but Hollywood continued to push the concepts of teenage independence and jovial lifestyle with the 1973 release of George Lucas's *American Graffiti*, the movie credited with jumpstarting the revival of 1950s-themed entertainment. This nostalgia was seen not only in the release of movies such as *The Great Gatsby* (1975) and *At Long Last Love* (1975), but also in television shows such as *Happy Days* (1974-1984) and *Laverne and Shirley* (1976-1988). Everything that was old became new again.

Combined, the 1980s and 90s introduced numerous genres that displayed certain characteristics of what was now a well established demographic. Teen sex comedies such as *Porky's* (1982) and *American Pie* (1999) dealt very openly and vulgarly with the theme of sexual coming-of-age, while carrying through the "adult vs. teens" motif which had begun in the 50s. Horror flicks such as *Nightmare on Elm Street* (1984) and *Scream* (1996) sent the message that parents cannot help, and that teenagers must stick together if they are going to conquer their fears, re-emphasizing the "us vs. them" mentality. Films such as *The Breakfast Club* (1985) and *Titanic* (1997) focused on teen angst, and treated the various issues teenagers face - love, abandonment, acceptance – as legitimate, despite adult characters' presumed perception of these issues as trivial.

As the 21st century has kicked off, Hollywood has continued to introduce teen movies that present progressively adult themes and situations. Following with the opening disclaimer of the 1950s *Blackboard Jungle*, film studios continue to argue that their movies simply reflect attitudes and lifestyles already present in current culture. I would agree that as society has changed and become more openly immoral, what we've seen and heard in movies has done the same. However, we don't have to look too far past the trends of fashion, relationships, attitudes, and political views to realize that there is a cycle at work, and that Hollywood and those who produce movies have an impact on society's thoughts, including those of our teenagers.

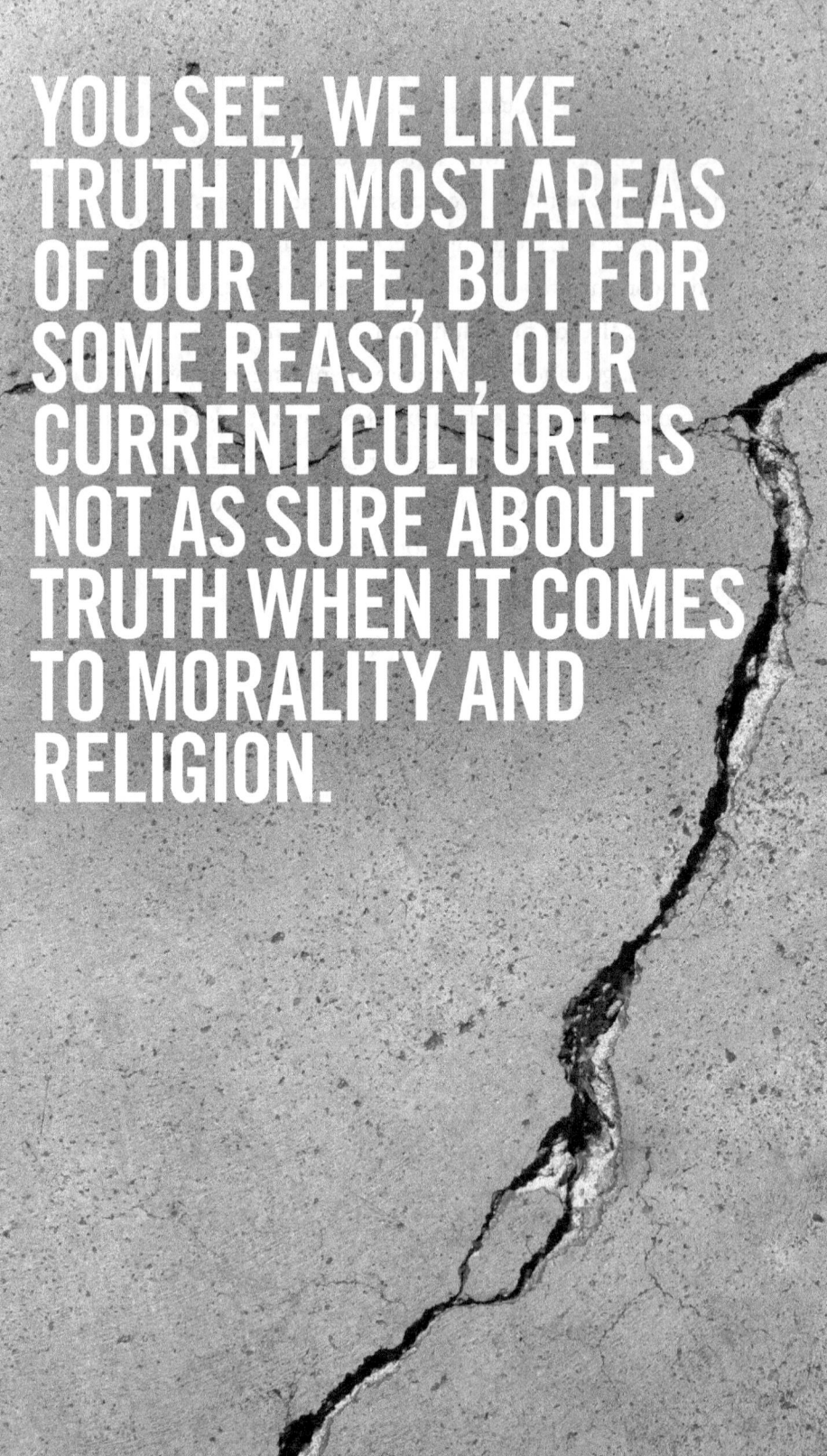

YOU SEE, WE LIKE TRUTH IN MOST AREAS OF OUR LIFE, BUT FOR SOME REASON, OUR CURRENT CULTURE IS NOT AS SURE ABOUT TRUTH WHEN IT COMES TO MORALITY AND RELIGION.

CHAPTER 3

THE CRACK IN THE FOUNDATION

"As a kid, you don't know any better. But then as you go on, the cracks begin to appear and you're like, I'm not sure about this hell thing. And I'm not sure whether it's really wrong to be gay, and I'm not sure whether we're right and they're wrong." [1]

– Chris Martin, lead singer of *Coldplay*

His name is Derek. When we met, I was 19 or 20 years old, working as part of a volunteer youth team at my local congregation. Derek was about 12 years old at the time. He was a great, outgoing kid with all the leadership qualities that any youth worker would want. If we needed a volunteer in class, Derek was one of the first to raise his hand. When we were at a retreat, I didn't have to spend time worrying about him getting into trouble. He was very well-behaved and just an all-around good kid.

Obeying the Gospel was a natural step for him as he grew up with Christian parents and regularly attended worship, Bible classes, and youth group activities. He would lead singing when the congregation invited young men to do so, and he participated in national conventions where he won awards for song leading and his speaking ability. He was a leader and an active Christian young man. It definitely wasn't a lack of involvement that led to his guest appearance on my national podcast in December of 2010.

GAME PLAN

As the years progressed, Derek and I lost track of each other. I became a full-time youth minister at another congregation. Although I saw Derek at a few youth events and he would come join us during our Bible studies on occasions, our times together became less and less frequent.

Eventually, I came back into contact with Derek on Facebook, when I read a few of his posts about a protest he was heavily involved with at a local university. The protest was initiated because the university had fired its head women's soccer coach after she informed her team that she and her partner, who happened to be another woman, were having a child together. At that time, the university had a strong policy against this sort of thing, so their response was swift. However, so was the response of Derek and those who had decided they would stand up for the rights of the coach.

The fact that Derek, a Christian, was on the front lines and instrumental in helping organize such an event was eye opening to me. There have been Christians who have stood up for the rights of others for some time; however, once I started paying closer attention to the videos that were being published to Facebook, it became very evident that this protest wasn't simply about the university's decision. Rather, it was advocating the advancement of the homosexual agenda, promoting the world's acceptance of this lifestyle.

I didn't understand how Derek, the "youth group all-star", had become a major organizer of a pro-homosexual rally. I knew he would be a leader in whatever he wanted to pursue, but I had never expected him to take this route. There had to be a lesson that parents and youth workers needed to learn from this young man, so I invited him on *The Hey Joe Show* one night to be interviewed. I really didn't know where the conversation would end up. That's why when I heard Derek say he no longer considered himself a Christian, my heart sank and my desire to help – both Derek and those listening to the podcast – took over.

JOE: *Let me ask you this, though, brother, because you bring to light something. Based upon your statement, even though you grew up in the church of Christ, you obeyed the Gospel, would you call yourself a Christian today?*

DEREK: *Oh, no. No, I would not.*

JOE: *What would you call yourself then? Are you an atheist? Are you an agnostic? What are you?*

DEREK: *I'd call myself an atheist agnostic humanist. I'm going to break that down some for you, because it sounds like two contradictory terms there, atheist and agnostic. Atheist means I don't believe there is a God. Agnostic means I don't for a fact know that there is or is not a God as the same way you don't know for a fact that there is and there is not a God. You have to have faith and trust in the belief of it. But it's humanist in the way that I have a faith in humanity, that in the end humans will for the most part do the right thing and realize what needs to be done to progress as a society.*

Sadly, Derek represents thousands of young people who have decided that the "old-religion" of their parents isn't truly where they need to be, leaving a multitude of parents weeping and wondering where they went wrong. Research shows that across the religious board, approximately 75 percent to 90 percent of teens walk out on their faith background when they graduate high school. The lessons that were taught, the sermons that were preached, the fellowship with others in the youth group become regarded merely as something that ignorant children participate in because their parents made them. When the foundation of their faith is attacked, it too often is truly as Chris Martin's quote at the opening of this chapter states: "…the cracks begin to appear."

But why do they appear, and where are the attacks coming from?

GAME PLAN

THE GREAT QUESTION

In John 18, we read of how Jesus was paraded before the Jewish high priest, the high priest's father-in-law, and ultimately, Pontius Pilot. After the rooster's crow caught the apostle Peter in his third denial, the writer brought the scene to Jesus in front of the Roman procurator. It's during this interrogation that we read the following:

> *36 "Jesus answered, 'My kingdom is not of this world. If My kingdom were of this world, then My servants would be fighting so that I would not be handed over to the Jews; but as it is, My kingdom is not of this realm.' 37 Therefore Pilate said to Him, 'So You are a king?' Jesus answered, 'You say correctly that I am a king. For this I have been born, and for this* **I have come into the world, to testify to the truth**. *Everyone who is of the truth hears My voice." (emphasis added)*

Pilate then asked Jesus a simple question, one that echoes even to this day.

> *38 "What is truth?"*

The difficulty of this question is reflected not only in Derek's perspective, but in the thousands of teens who this very year will decide to walk away from their Lord and Savior. Without an answer, they wander into the land of humanism, where all trust is placed in the individual, where intellectual elitists reign, and where the bashing of all authority related to moral truth takes over.

The question of truth has been asked numerous times throughout history, and it brings much controversy; however, this controversy seems to be reserved mainly for areas of religion and morality. We seek out truth from a doctor, and usually take his or her diagnosis as accurate. Even when we seek a different opinion, ultimately we trust in a doctor knowing truth when it comes to health. When financial planners tell us how our investments are performing, we take their word for it because we know they are looking at the evidence before they ever make the statement. When you look at the ingredients on the back of a can of soup, you trust the manufacturers are giving you truth when it comes to what's inside their product. You see, we like truth in most areas of our life, but for some reason, our current culture is not as sure about truth when it comes to morality and religion.

DRESSING ROOMS DON'T LIE

In life, there are a few places we all go where truth is revealed. A dressing room is one of those places. We walk in with multiple pieces of clothing, hoping that something will fit just right and look half-decent. Sometimes we have to bump up a size or choose another color to find what that works for us. Whatever the case, once you step into that dressing room, you will come out with the truth of what works and what doesn't.

In our society, many people are treating truth the same way they treat the shopping experience. We go into the "outlet mall" of current culture and shop the racks, buying whatever we want. In a land where 93 percent of the citizens profess a belief in Christianity[2], one would think the Bible would reign supreme; however, in our current culture, it does not. When only 16 percent of adults claim they make decisions based upon the Bible and only 35 percent claim that truth is absolute, there is inconsistency in what we say we believe and what we actually believe.[3] If this is the example that we show the majority of teens, should it really shock us that three out of four don't believe we can know absolute truth?

The question must be asked: How did we get here? When did we stop existing as a "Christian" nation and begin living as a humanistic society? It is written of the children of Israel,

> "In those days there was no king in Israel; everyone did what was right in his own eyes." (Judges 21:25)

GAME PLAN

What we are facing today is nothing new; however, the major difference is that when the Israelites turned from God, they would often turn toward a foreign god. Today, America does the same; however, our god is self. We have turned our backs on scriptures such as Proverbs 14:12:

> *"There is a way that seems right to a man, but its end is the way of death."*

Many believe that truth is based upon feelings, and so truth can change with each circumstance. To understand how this perspective came about, let's take a quick look at where we've been.

PRE-MODERN – (Creation - 1700s)

This period of time is marked by a strong belief in the supernatural realm. God (or gods) exercised absolute authority and had power over all areas. Truth was considered to be outside of man and in the power of God (or gods) and this authority was unquestioned by most. Prophets, priests, shamans, or witchdoctors taught about God (or gods) to those who would listen. Truth was present, and it was found in a Being higher than man.

MODERN – (1700s -1960s)

Human understanding and the race of science fueled movements such as The Enlightenment and the Industrial Revolution. It was through the many advances in science that some began to believe humanity was limitless in what it could do to bring about positive change and make a better world for all. Knowledge itself became the idol worshiped and man's reason and logic began to replace divine revelation or reliance upon God (or gods).

CRACK IN THE FOUNDATION

POST-MODERN – (1960s – Current)

November 22, 1963 is the date some ascribe to the beginning of this period. The assassination of John F. Kennedy and the Vietnam War led many Americans, especially younger Americans, to realize that the promises of the Modern period had not come to fruition. Death, destruction, and disease, alongside poverty, pollution, and politics, all played a major role in the seismic shift from optimism to hopelessness. There was and continues to be a rejection of the systems, laws, traditions, and principles of the past periods, and an acceptance that there really are no absolute truths. Decisions are made on "gut instincts" and the slogan "this is a free country" is spouted often when anyone makes a statement of absolute truth, especially against any immoral behavior. We live in a time when attitudes of "you can't be so judgmental" and "how dare you push your beliefs on me" roam the streets and sit in some of the most powerful seats in our nation.

Current culture declares the only absolute truth is that we absolutely can't know anything for sure. However, such declarations do not stop truth from existing. Unlike going into a dressing room to try on clothes, where you leave with what fits you, truth is not dependent upon us. In the dressing room, if we try on a shirt that doesn't fit, we can go out and find another shirt that does. However, truth is outside of us, objective in nature. If it doesn't fit, it's not because there's something wrong with the truth; instead, there is something truth-seekers must change about themselves. Truth is based on the One who is Truth, Jesus Christ, and He does not change (John 1:14).

ABSOLUTE TRUTH VS. RELATIVE TRUTH

Stephen, a hard-working man, finds himself on the bottom end of the economic ladder. Every day he wakes up and heads to the factory before 5AM. Holding his dull metal lunchbox, he kisses his wife and children goodbye and steps out the door for a long day of hard labor.

One day, as Stephen comes through the door, something is different. Instead of rushing in to hug his family, he stands at the door. He appears defeated and broken as he explains to his wife that with cut-backs in effect, there is simply no work at the factory for him, and he has been laid off. As she wonders how they will pay the bills and feed the children, Stephen slouches in his chair, feeling like less than a man, not able to provide.

He leaves the next morning to look for work, only to have doors slammed in his face. He stands in the unemployment line day after day, but there's not enough money to make ends meet. At home, the electricity is turned off, bill collectors call at all hours of the day and night, food is scarce... and Stephen sinks further into darkness.

The next day, Stephen comes home with a bag full of apples. As his wife stares in amazement, the children rush over; with smiles on their faces, they each grab an apple and take a big, juicy bite. After the children leave the room, Stephen sits down and answers his wife's questions. No, he had not gotten a new job. No, in fact, he had not paid for the food. He explains that while walking by the grocery store, he saw no one looking, and so he grabbed a bag full of apples from the sidewalk and just kept walking.

Stop the tape! – Was Stephen, a poor man in hard times, justified in doing this? His children have to eat, don't they? Was he right in taking the apples?

Many in our current culture have fallen into the pit of relative truth, where situational ethics rule. They claim that right and wrong is dependent on the circumstance; therefore, we can't look at every situation through the same lens. People of this mindset might reason that for most individuals, stealing is definitely not the right thing to do; however, for a man in Stephen's predicament, it is absolutely justified. They might even go as far to say that he did the right thing.

How do we know when something is right or wrong? Is it really left up to a subjective truth, to be determined by the person in the situation, or is there truth that exists for all people in all cultures at all times?

In my interview with Derek, I sought to better understand his thought

MARKETING TO TEENS

process on this subject of relative and absolute truth. While I could have simply asked him very pointedly what he thought about the subject, I took an approach that would demonstrate the thought process of many who profess a belief in relative truth. Notice in the dialogue below how Derek's standard for right and wrong shifts from self, to the law of the land, and ultimately back to self.

> **DEREK:** *No, I'm not a practicing homosexual. I've never been. I just feel that it's a basic human rights issue, and I feel like everybody has to- has the right to have the same opportunities that I'm afforded. I don't think we should be prejudiced against anybody just for the way that they choose to live their life or make themselves happy.*

> **JOE:** *You just made a pretty strong statement that everyone deserves to have that right. Do you feel the same way about pedophiles?*

> **DEREK:** *Now, I think that you're drawing a line here on what do I feel is the morality of homosexuality as opposed to pedophiles, and I think it's pretty obvious, you know, pedophiles are preying on people who are below the age of consent. They're people who aren't old enough to make decisions for themselves and can easily be taken advantage of. So no, a pedophile is a very different, completely different beast than homosexuality. I don't think anybody would disagree with me there.*

> **JOE:** *So if there was a 16 year old who has the ability to make a decision about consensual sex with a 30 year old man, you would view that as still something that that individual with a 16 year old would not have the right to have sex with that person?*

> **DEREK:** *With a 32 year old man?*

> **JOE:** *Sure.*

GAME PLAN

DEREK: I mean, we can look to the laws of our own judicial system to see that that would be wrong.

JOE: So you would say that if the laws say something is wrong, then it's wrong?

DEREK: I would - I would say that in this particular case, yes, that is the case.

JOE: How do you draw a distinction, and who draws the lines as far as what is acceptable and what is not?

DEREK: Well, currently, our lawmakers draw the line with what is acceptable and what is not. I think each of us has our own ethical duty to find what we feel is morally right and wrong, and I think we can draw our own personal lines. But I don't know - beyond that, I think - what exactly are you trying to ask me beyond that?

JOE: Well, I guess my question is, and this is something that obviously, it's beyond religion. It goes to a core morality. If we're going to start drawing lines of what can and can't be, which is what I understand what the rally was about was individuals upset at what Belmont did, practicing their right to draw a line as an institution. There were people that were unhappy where that line was drawn. And I guess when we look at morality, when we look at civil rights, as you called it, and we'll deal with that here in a second, who has the right to draw the line? I mean, after all, if I say homosexuality is a sin, therefore, it should not be practiced, I would be looked at as judgmental. But in the same sense, if somebody said that a human having sex with an animal is grotesque, well, my question is, where do they draw that line? What is the basis of their line that they just drew in the sand to say that an individual could not have sex with an animal?

CRACK IN THE FOUNDATION

DEREK: *The basis for lines is based on personal moral beliefs. And then as for society, we get together and we decide by electing officials, who decide what our legal line is.*

JOE: *Now, in that same line, would you agree then, if it's set by society, if society passed the law that said it's okay for a 30 year old man to have sex with a 16 year old, then it would be okay based on society saying it was okay?*

DEREK: *This is a really hypothetical question you're asking me here. But secondly, the moral code still is there, despite whatever the laws are. In your own self, you know whether something's right or wrong.*

When it comes to the subject of absolute truth and subjective (relative) truth, the key is really on the standard used to determine right and wrong. If left up each individual, truth will always fluctuate. It will change when the cost of the outcome might be more than someone is willing to pay. In some situations, if children are involved, emotions can take over and leave behind a logical conclusion.

The only way to truly answer questions of truth is to have a way to test these truths to determine if they are absolute. That test must compare actions and attitudes to a standard of right and wrong; that standard must exist separate, above, and beyond our culture and ourselves. Just as the International Bureau of Weights and Measurements standardizes units of measure, making a meter the same in Oklahoma as it is in Kenya, we must find the same when it comes to truth. We must be willing to compare what we think the truth is to the Original Standard who is common to all humanity, to all creation.

What is the Standard? Who or what exist outside of any human culture? Who or what exists outside of a time restriction and outside of us as humans? Friends, there's only one who fits every single one of those qualifications – God. He is the Standard. As Moses penned in Deuteronomy 32,

GAME PLAN

> *4 "The Rock! His work is perfect,*
> *For all His ways are just;*
> *A God of faithfulness and without injustice,*
> *Righteous and upright is He."*

So let's go back to Stephen- was he right or wrong? Using God as my Standard, it is never right to do the wrong thing, even if the right outcome is achieved. Regardless of your culture or time, taking something that belongs to someone else without trading or paying is always wrong (see Exodus 20:15; Ephesians 4:28). Stealing from another, regardless of the reason, devalues the other person as the thief elevates his needs or wants above those of another person. After all, like all truth, this goes back to the nature of God as "the Rock".

THE ILLOGICAL LOGIC

Have you ever met someone who would argue with a tree if they thought the tree had an opinion different from their own? Maybe you've discussed a very serious topic with a friend of yours, only to discover during the course of the conversation that he couldn't possibly be listening to his own words, because his statements simply didn't make any sense. When you encounter someone with postmodern beliefs – there is no such thing as absolute truth - many times, that's exactly what happens. Postmodernists' claims, often times with an "intellectual backing" ("Dr. Smith said it; therefore, it must be so") are not based upon simple logic, but rather on feelings. It's a thought process with this predetermined conclusion as the main driving force: that all standard of right and wrong are obviously judgmental and therefore, evil.

Consider a few of the illogical logic statements that are made in defense of relative truth.

CRACK IN THE FOUNDATION

Claim 1: "There are no absolutes."

I love it when someone makes an absolute statement about there not being any absolutes. How do they know their statement is true, and if their statement is true, does that make it an absolute truth? The postmodern thinker would say "No", which again, is an absolute statement.

Claim 2: "Truth is relative."

Really?? In order to make this claim, the individual has to use an absolute statement to say that truth is not absolute. Does that sound more than a little illogical to anyone else? Also, if truth is relative, then it would stand to reason that this statement is not always true – if it's not relative to my truth.

Claim 3: "No one knows what the truth is."

How can a person know this statement is true if no one knows what is truth? If a person is going to make this claim, by default they are making a statement that they are claiming is true. It's illogical to say this.

Claim 4: "It's wrong for you to impose your morals on me."

By making this claim, the speaker is attempting to impose his or her morals on the hearer. Telling me that my actions or beliefs are wrong is not only a judgment, but it is an attempt to change my morals when it comes to speaking against immorality.

Claim 5: "Everybody can believe whatever they want!"

If this statement is true, then why do relativists argue in the first place? Why would they try to make you see the argument their way if your way – even if you believe they are wrong – is correct as well? In a day of tolerance of all viewpoints, it's amazing to hear intolerance being exposed in the "let's tolerate everyone" camp. What they really mean is that you are free to believe what you want, unless you believe that they are wrong. If

GAME PLAN

you believe they are wrong, they will try to convince you to change. Once again – an illogical claim.

WHERE'S THIS COMING FROM?

As you can imagine, during my conversation with Derek I wanted to learn as much as I could about the change that had taken place in his thought process. Knowing the Derek of old and comparing him with the new Derek, I needed to know what changed. What happened to the knowledge he received in Bible classes and at youth functions, much less the teaching he received from his Christian parents? The answer is a lesson that every elder, deacon, minister, and – most importantly – every parent needs to hear.

> **JOE:** ... But the question that I have, if you don't mind kind of addressing it, is through your teaching, growing up through various youth programs, various Bible classes and whatnot, did the subject of homosexuality, was it ever addressed? As you were growing up in the Church, was there ever a teaching about homosexuality and the way the Bible views it?
>
> **DEREK:** Of course homosexuality was stressed. There was a lot of mention of the Old Testament verses condemning homosexuality, and there was a lot of hinting that the New Testament condemned homosexuality. But it was a lot of rhetoric, a lot of people talking about their feelings and the sentiments of it and less, I guess, quoting of Scriptures from the New Testament.
>
> **JOE:** Gotcha. So you felt at that stage that maybe it wasn't addressed in an appropriate manner, but it was just looked at as, well, those are just religious people talking?

CRACK IN THE FOUNDATION

DEREK: *Well, I mean, at the time when I was told this, of course I believed it like anybody who goes to Bible classes. We wouldn't go if we didn't believe in the things that we're being taught. But it was later in life through my own personal studying that I realized that, you know, maybe the Bible doesn't say as much especially in the New Testament about homosexuality as particularly the church of Christ doctrine would say it does.*

JOE: *When did you dive into your own studies to come to the conclusion that you've come to today to be on the front lines of pushing the LGBT civil rights, as you called it, their rights? When did you transition? How did that transition take place? What was it that came about that you said, wait a minute, maybe I've had this wrong all this time?*

DEREK: *Well, as I mentioned earlier, I started going to Belmont. But it was from actually learning in their Biblical classes about - I had an Old Testament class and a New Testament class.* **And they were really instrumental in me coming to my current beliefs** *because they really dove into a lot of the historical facts of things, talking about the different filters that we view the Bible from. The Bible's a really ancient document. It was written in the Bronze Ages, the Old Testament was. And it was more in the sense of a national epic, kind of like "Beowulf." And then the New Testament, the gospels are of course written in the Roman Greco biography style, and then the letters from Paul, quote, unquote, letters was the style. So I think we first have to have a lot of different layers of understanding of the Bible. And I think it was a tool set that they gave me, and a way to study religion and other documents that really allowed me to form my own beliefs. (emphasis added)*

Through his response, Derek revealed so much when it comes to how this moral relativism begins and where, in far too many cases, the attacks take place. As he walked out the door as an incoming college freshman – he believed in the credibility of the Bible and what was taught in the

GAME PLAN

context of his Bible classes. When he walked through another door as a college graduate – he believed the absolute opposite. At this particular school, one that has a religious background to it, the professors were able to destroy in his mind the very foundation of his morals and values that his parents spent 18 years instilling in him.

Once the credibility of the Bible was attacked, they went after the existence of God. By teaching him the Theory of Evolution as factual, the professors indoctrinated Derek with the idea that to believe in God was simply a comforting thought for those who did not seek after facts.

> **JOE:** ...From an atheist standpoint, how do you then handle the issue of if there is a design, then there must be a designer? How would you respond to that?
>
> **DEREK:** That's kind of an argument from ignorance there. We're saying that since obviously things exist, there must be someone who designed them. Just because of the complexity of something doesn't mean that it had to result from a supernatural being creating it. I think that you're way off here on what you're basing it on. So it's like, well, if this exists, there must be a God. There's no other reason for everything. It couldn't have just happened by chance. But you know, while this might seem like a very comforting idea, that we will always be around in some sort of sense, I think it comes down to are you really searching for what's the truth, or are you really searching for what comforts you, what makes you feel good. **And eventually, I decided that I wasn't looking for something just to pacify me, to placate me. I wanted something that was truthful, that was backed up by factual statements.** It's hard for me to believe something like the Tower of Babel, for instance, all languages stemming from one language, when we know that that's absolutely not how language developed in the world, you know. It's just kind of an absurd idea that all languages came about in a day instead of developing in the way that they did, or at least that the ancient

CRACK IN THE FOUNDATION

languages came about all in one day and everybody just woke up one day speaking another tongue. There's too many -- I mean, I just kind of got tired of the apologetics of it. (emphasis added)

I wanted to know how a Christian "youth group all-star" could go from being on fire for the Lord to standing on the front lines of a pro-homosexual rally and working for a LGBT magazine. The answer: with the credibility of the Bible removed and the need for God negated by the teaching of evolution, morality and values were left up to the individual to determine. The professors successfully, at least in the life of Derek, kicked God off the throne and placed man in His place – the very essence of what humanism truly is. The overwhelmingly sad fact is that this is happening year after year, and many well-meaning parents are literally paying for it.

Nearly 30 years ago, in a publication entitled *The Humanist*, author John Dunphy defined the battle lines in this war when he wrote:

> *I am convinced that the battle for humankind's future must be waged and won in the public school classroom by teachers who correctly perceive their role as the proselytizers of a new faith: a religion of humanity that recognizes and respects the spark of what theologians call divinity in every human being. These teachers must embody the same selfless dedication as the most rabid fundamentalist preachers, for* **they will be ministers of another sort, utilizing a classroom instead of a pulpit to convey humanist values in whatever subject they teach**, *regardless of the educational level – preschool day care or large state university. The classroom must and will become an arena of conflict between the old and the new – the rotting corpse of Christianity, together with all its adjacent evils and misery, and the new faith of humanism.*[4] *(emphasis added)*

While not every teacher at a preschool day care or a large state university adheres to the propaganda pushed by Dunphy, there are plenty who do. Those who do not hold this belief are often looked down upon or even blacklisted, as exposed in Ben Stein's documentary *Expelled: No Intelligence Allowed*. As the American education system has moved further away from a religious foundation, secularists – those who believe the government and all entities run by the government should operate without any religious beliefs – have continued to push the envelope in all areas and in every subject that is taught. The current idea of "rule by majority" that the secular humanist's advocate is becoming more and more commonplace as college students return home for the summer and explain their new beliefs to the very parents who spent the first 18 years of their lives teaching them about Abraham, Isaac, Jacob, Paul, Peter, and Jesus Christ.

Professors such as Richard Rorty, who taught at Wellesley, Princeton, the University of Virginia and Stanford are more than happy to replace the teachings that his students received at home. Speaking on behalf of humanistic professors, Rorty has said,

> "We are going to go right on trying to discredit you in the eyes of your children, trying to strip your fundamentalist religious community of dignity, trying to make your views seem silly rather than discussable... arrange things so that students who enter as bigoted, homophobic religious fundamentalists will leave college with views more like our own."[3]

Plenty of Rorty's fellow professors have boldly claimed the same:

In a recent study entitled *How Religious are America's College and University Professors*, authors Neil Gross and Solon Simmons discovered the true climate in America's universities. Desiring a balanced approach, they set out to correct false or biased information that had been spread through previous reports. They discovered that, on the whole, college professors are less religious than other Americans:

CRACK IN THE FOUNDATION

- **23.4%** *of college professors claim to be atheists or agnostics.*
- **19.6%** *of college professors claim they believe in a Higher Power, but not a personal God.*
- **4.4%** *of college professors claim to believe in God some of the time but not at others.*
- **16.9%** *of college professors claim they have many doubts, but that they do believe in God.*
- **6.1%** *of college professors believe the Bible is the "actual word of God."*
- **51.6%** *of college professors believe the Bible is "an ancient book of fables, legends, history, and moral precepts."*
- **33.9%** *of college professors claim they are "not religious".*
- **75.1%** *of college professors said that religion does not belong in public schools, and that public schools should not be allowed to start each day with a public prayer.*
- **84.1%** *of college professors disagreed that Intelligent Design is a serious scientific alternative to the Darwinian theory of evolution.*[11]

Our current culture insists that without a college degree from a major university, young people will never achieve the same success in life as their contemporaries who did earn a degree. This fear drives many parents to push their children to get into a well-respected college. Sometimes the teens aren't even sure if the college degree is their own goal or the goal of their parents, but either way, to please their parents and adhere to current culture, teens decide college is the step they must take after high school.

Why? Why is this considered the next step that must be taken?

Parents, let me pose to you a serious thought: Imagine a pit full of deadly snakes. If your child can survive inside this pit for four years, she will receive a huge monetary reward. However, you know that if your child enters the pit, odds are two out of three that she will be bitten and

GAME PLAN

subsequently die. Would you grab your child and throw her in the pit, thinking of the reward she could potentially earn? What if the odds were improved to "only" a 50/50 chance that she might die? Would you throw her into the pit now? I would even go this far – what if the odds were improved in your child's favor- there is just a one out of three chance of being bitten and dying? Would you throw her in with those odds? Most of you are shaking your heads right now and saying "No!" emphatically. You would never risk the life of your child for something as trivial as dollars and cents. You couldn't imagine going through the rest of this life without your precious child.

Prof. Michael Berube Professor of English, Penn State University	*"In the class, we talk about what it means to be an 'anti-foundationalist' – that is, one of those sane, secular people who believe that it's best to operate as if our moral and epistemological principles derive not from divine will or uniform moral law, but from ordinary social practices."*[6]
Prof. Timothy Shortell Associate Professor of Sociology, Brooklyn College	*"[R]eligion without fantacism is a logical impossibility. Anyone whose mind is trapped inside such a mental prison will be susceptible to extreme forms of hatred and violence. Faith is, by its very nature, obsessive-compulsive. All religions foment their own kind of holy war."*[7]
Prof. Thomas Sugrue Professor of History and Sociology, University of Pennsylvania	religion is *"the subject of distrust and even derision...much of the academic skepticism about organized religion is warranted."*[8]
Prof. Peter Singer Professor of Bioethics, Princeton University	*"If we don't play God, who will? There seem to me to be three possibilities: there is a God, but He doesn't care about evil and suffering; there is a God who cares, but He or She is a bit of an underachiever; or there is no God. Personally, I believe the latter."*[9]

CRACK IN THE FOUNDATION

Prof. Steven Weinberg
Physics and Astronomy Department, University of Texas

"I think in many respects religion is a dream – a beautiful dream often. Often a nightmare, but it's a dream from which I think it's about time we awoke. Just as a child learns about the tooth fairy and is incited by that to leave a tooth under the pillow – and you're glad that the child believes in the tooth fairy. But eventually you want the child to grow up."[10]

Friend, why then, just because current culture claims it to be the case, do we automatically assume the next step after high school for our children needs to be a degree from a major university? Right now, your child's chance of entering a snake pit and surviving is better than his odds of entering into a major university and coming out after four years as a faithful Christian. I'm not a "throw the baby out with the bath water" guy; however, I refuse to live in a make-believe world. Satan puts serious dangers in the world for our children, and we must first and foremost understand that our #1 desire for our children must be that they are faithful followers of Jesus Christ – not that they get "the great job".

After recognizing the dangers, and in order combat them, we must weigh what alternatives are out there.

THE ALTERNATIVES

Alternative #1

Let me suggest to you that of the two, Christian or Secular, the Christian colleges are a better option. No, not every professor at a Christian college is faithful to the Lord, as was discovered by Gross and Simmons; nor do all Christian colleges hold to the same standard of truth. However, I propose to you that they are a better option because at the core the Bible is still revered, and the vast majority of the professors strongly believe in the existence of God and His authority in our lives. The hope is that the atmosphere surrounding the campus will be one where spiritually minded individuals roam, making it easier for your child to walk in the Light in every area.

Does that mean the colleges will be perfect or that every professor will be the positive spiritual mentor your child latches on to when she is there? Not necessarily, but the likelihood of that happening improves at a Christian college.

Alternative #2

Another, albeit less prestigious, option that offers your teen a better chance at remaining faithful, is the community college route. With this as an option, your teen will stay closer to home allowing you to have a stronger influence in their life as they begin transitioning out from under your roof. Their family ties will remain strong, which ultimately, will help them when their faith is attacked.

Alternative #3

A third option that will likely become much more prominent in the future as tuition soars, is taking college courses online. Again, your teen lives either in your house or close to family, providing strength and mentorship as they continue to grow. The overall cost for this type of schooling decreases tremendously without room and board expenses. Options Two and Three also allow your teen to stay connected with the church, not searching for a new congregation that believes and worships as God instructs through His Word.

Alternative #4

Lastly, I would state to you that most teens graduate high school knowing enough to get into college, and many have SAT or ACT scores that earn them scholarships; but most do not know enough from the Bible to be able to withstand the attacks Satan will throw at them. One option that many don't consider, but that is available to both young men and young women, is enrollment in a school of preaching to gain a more solid foundation. Most of these programs are only two years, so it doesn't consume as much time. Also, if your child does want to transfer to a Christian college after completing a school of preaching program, most Christian colleges will accept transfer credits. This final method is less expensive and offers a way to further ground your teen in the Word and, ultimately, in their faith.

CHALK TALK: WHAT'S THE GAME PLAN?

1) Take responsibility when it comes to grounding your children in the Word of God.

Most Christian parents do a great job teaching the "stories" of the Bible. However, this can present a problem if the accounts in the Bible are then forever looked at as "stories" instead of true situations, in which people truly struggled and truly trusted in God. Parents, the responsibility to teach your children is first and foremost on your shoulders, and it goes beyond just teaching on-the-surface topics. Derek was taught what the Bible said; however, when his faith was challenged, the foundation crumbled. Ensure that you are prepared to teach your children the credibility of the Bible, the existence of God, and the credibility of Jesus. These will be the first lines of attack when they leave your house. If their foundation cracks, their values, ethics, and morals will eventually follow.

GAME PLAN

2) Help your teen decide what the next step is after high school.

Many in our society claim that when a child is 18, they are adults who, like birds learning to fly, should be kicked out of the nest, but is this a Biblical approach? I'm not recommending sheltering them or preventing them from growing up; however, fathers and mothers need to remember that the 18 year old doesn't have everything figured out yet (although many 18 year olds might say otherwise!). Encourage them to consider the other options. If the spiritual reasons aren't enough to persuade them, maybe the reasons relating to money will. Most importantly, help your teen fight the "culture says it – so I will do it" mentality.

3) Teach by your words and your life that the number one goal is heaven.

If the only message your children see in your life or hears from you is that success is measured by the job one has and the amount of money one makes, then they will live their lives in pursuit of that goal. However, if you show them that your #1 goal is heaven, and that you use your job and money to progress toward that goal, they will pursue that instead.

Have no doubt: the attack on truth will happen in their lives. Don't give your children a reason to pursue the wrong things, leaving eternity with God in heaven behind.

CRACK IN THE FOUNDATION

STRAIGHT TALK WITH TEENS

To hear the entire interview with Derek as heard on
The Hey Joe Show visit
www.TheEquipNetwork.com.

REGARDLESS OF THEIR RATIONALE, GOD DID NOT SIT IDLY BY AND CONTINUE BLESSING A PEOPLE WHO REFUSED TO GRANT HIM THE POSITION OF AUTHORITY IN THEIR LIVES.

CHAPTER 4:

WHAT DID WE REALLY THINK WOULD HAPPEN?

As you look further into the concept of absolute truth, consider how things have changed over the years. Even the ACT, an achievement test used to determine the academic qualifications of potential college students, was revised in 2005 to place a heavier interest on creative writing versus math and science. In the study guide published by Kaplan that year, it was said, *"What's important is that you take a position and state how you feel. It is not important what other people might think, just what you think."*

When we read this, it sounds nice. After all, young people on the brink of adulthood should be able to think for themselves, and must also be able to express their thoughts verbally and in writing. However, stating that it doesn't matter what other people think teaches a lesson that the individual is the center of attention – we looked at it last chapter as putting mankind on the throne of truth, or the concept of "self" taking control and God being placed in the backseat.

Consider the book of Judges for a moment. The overall theme brings to mind the image of a rollercoaster with its ups and downs, highs and lows. When the children of Israel turned their trust and attention to Jehovah God, they were on a high point, and He would deliver them from bondage.

GAME PLAN

It's when they turned away from Him that they encountered slavery and hardships – representing the downward plummet of the rollercoaster. The book of Judges is truly a continual ride of highs and lows, twist and turns.

The opening chapter of Judges relays God's commands about the conquest of Canaan, the land promised to Abraham. The mission was simple: take possession of all the land and drive out the inhabitants. Over and over again, we learn of Israel's deliberate failure to do what God had instructed as they allowed the pagan people to live in the land along with them; they even failed to conquer some of the territories. With this occurring in the first chapter, we really shouldn't be surprised by what we read at the beginning of Chapter 2:

> *1 "Now the angel of the Lord came up from Gilgal to Bochim. And he said, 'I brought you up out of Egypt and led you into the land which I have sworn to your fathers; and I said, 'I will never break my covenant with you, and as for you, you shall make no covenant with the inhabitants of this land; you shall tear down their altars.' But you have not obeyed Me; what is this you have done?"*

Surely the children of Israel didn't think that God would be ignorant of their disobedience! How foolish could they be? Didn't they know their own history? Although many of these individuals would not have been alive during the time when God used Moses to lead the exodus from Egypt, they would have heard about His power demonstrated through the plagues and the parting of the Red Sea. They would have seen the power of God at Jericho and would have known of Him as they followed Joshua. So how could they think disobeying God, and instead doing what they wanted to do, was going to turn out well for them?

Regardless of their rationale, God did not sit idly by and continue blessing a people who refused to grant Him the position of authority in their lives. Consequences were inevitable; as Chapter 2 continues, we read,

WHAT DID WE REALY THINK WOULD HAPPEN?

> **3** "Therefore I also said, 'I will not drive them out before you; but they will become as thorns in your sides and their gods will be a snare to you."

When the angel of the Lord spoke these words, the Israelites lifted up their voices and wept. At that point, they understood that following their own desires has a cost. God informed them that this cost would come in two installments. First, the physical price: leaving enemies of God in the land of Canaan would be a thorn in the side of Israel. Second, the spiritual price: the gods of these nations would be a snare, forever holding them back in their relationship with the one true God.

Now that is an interesting concept: **if we don't obey God, we will have both spiritual consequences and physical consequences**. Are we so arrogant in the United States as to believe we can remove God's authority and place ourselves in His place without facing physical consequences? Do we truly think that, even with our sinfulness, we will never encounter physical difficulties in our own lives and in society as a whole? Is it logical to think that we can purge God from public institutions and instill in the minds of our children that we are here by chance without any spiritual consequences? Friend, I propose to you that in America we are already seeing consequences – both physical and spiritual – of trying to remove God from His throne.

THE NEW AMERICAN IDOL: SELF-ESTEEM

For Dr. Jene Twenge, professor of psychology at San Diego State University, the reference to today's generation of young people as "Millenials" or "Mosiacs" doesn't quite capture the true attitude and focus of this group. Twenge points out that this generation of people has been told all their lives how special they are, and they have genuinely bought into this idea. Today's teens believe that when they walk into a room, they deserve to be recognized. When two adults are talking, this current

> **Facebook Statistics:**[1]
> - More than **500 million** active users
> - **50%** of active users log on to Facebook in any given day
> - Average user has **130 friends**
> - People spend over **700 billion minutes per month** on Facebook
> - More than **70** translations available on the site
> - About **70%** of Facebook users are outside the United States
> - There are more than **250 million** active users currently accessing Facebook through their mobile devices.
> - People that use Facebook on their mobile devices are **twice as active** on Facebook than non-mobile users.

generation has been lead to believe that they have the right and are in the position to join in that conversation, interjecting their thoughts and feelings. Through outlets such as YouTube, UStream, Facebook, and Twitter, their thoughts and feelings are no longer reserved for their immediate circle of friends, but are broadcast across the globe. Why? Because our culture teaches us "everyone cares what my thoughts are… And even if someone doesn't actually care, I should still exercise my right to tell everyone what's on my mind."

The result? Dr. Twenge has termed this group "Generation Me", stating that **"…this generation has never known a world that put duty before self."** [2]

It's really hard to place all the blame for this on today's young generation. While today's young people score higher on self-esteem tests and are more assured of who they are and where they're going, this

WHAT DID WE REALY THINK WOULD HAPPEN?

is directly tied to aspects of American society. Whereas, the cultural movements of the 1960s and 70s sought for the first time to push towards self focus, still understanding a time in America where not only God was the focus, but so was the family and the country, Twenge explains all too well that those of Generation Me didn't have to work towards the elevation of self. They were born into a society that already celebrated the individual.

An increased push of self-esteem in the 1980s is well documented, when society for the first time made effort to heighten children's view of themselves. Magazines, television talk shows, and books all were used as mediums in this change as narcissism was the goal. In one children's book, entitled *The Lovables in the Kingdom of Self-Esteem*, the author penned,

"I AM LOVEABLE. Hi, lovable friend! My name is Mona Monkey. I live in the Kingdom of Self-Esteem along with my friends the Lovable Team." [3]

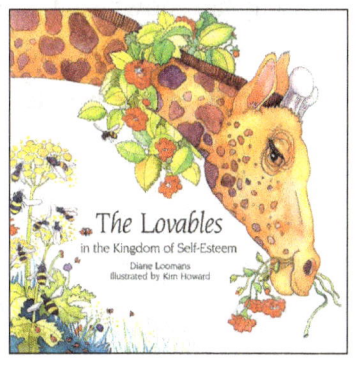

On the next page, the children learn that the gates of the "Kingdom of Self-Esteem" will burst open if you *"say these words three times with pride: I'm lovable! I'm lovable! I'm lovable!"* [4]

Other tools used in in the push of self-esteems during this time include the *Be a Winner Self-Esteem Coloring and Activity Book,* which contained a coloring page that simply said "YOU ARE SPECIAL" and a fill-in the blank activity page that read, "Accept y_ur_e_f. You're a special person. Use p_si_iv_ thinking". Programs such as the *Self-Science: The Subject Is Me* and *Pumsy in Pursuit of Excellence* were placed into the curriculum of many school districts across America, along with the "Magic Circle exercise", for which a child received a badge with the words inscribed "I'm Great!" Throughout the day, other children were to say positive and uplifting things about the one with the badge. At the end of the exercise, the child must then compliment himself. [5]

GAME PLAN

Children from the 50s and 60s gained self-esteem naturally in a stable environment that actually kept score during t-ball games; they learned that being a winner takes talent and hard work. Conversely, children from Generation Me, for the most part, have had their self-esteem artificially created. Their self-esteem is not based upon success and failure, strength of the family, or stability in society. Rather, in a culture where self-worship has become common place, their self-esteem comes from the fact that they are simply themselves. Society feared if a child's self-esteem was linked to performance, the child – being so brittle and frail – would be doomed to a life of failure when they inevitably did not perform well at some task. However, in the effort to protect our children, we actually created young people who do not handle negative feedback well at all. Study after study has shown that, when criticized, individuals with high self-esteem became unfriendly, rude, and uncooperative — leading researcher Dr. Roy Baumeister to conclude,

> *"It is very questionable whether [the few benefits] justify the effort and expense that schools, parents and therapists have put into raising self-esteem... After all these years, I'm sorry to say, my recommendation is this: forget about self-esteem and concentrate more on self-control and self-discipline."* [6]

The blame for this epidemic can only partially be placed on self-esteem curriculum in schools. Printed magazines, Internet social networking sites, radio, and the television contain advertisements that also pander to America's obsession with the "me" factor. Catchy marketing slogans have long served as a way to burn a brand in the minds of consumers; however, they also reflect society's wants, and today they drive the continued infatuation with self. Consider some of the most well-known slogans:

- *"Have it your way"* – Burger King
- *"Obey your thirst"* – Sprite
- *"Be your own rock"* – Prudential

CRACK IN THE FOUNDATION

- *"An Army of One"* – U.S. Army
- *"Because I'm worth it"* - L'Oreal
- *"Fly your own flag"* - New Era Caps
- *"Your journey, our passion"* – Bridgestone

Finally, the responsibility for the elevation of the individual as most important rests on the shoulders of parents. Understand that I would never suggest to you that a child with healthy self-esteem is an evil person; nor would I ever suggest we need to belittle our children so they have low self-esteem. Rather, I ask you to consider reality: what difficulties will your child encounter when she is out of your house and in the work force, or staying at home as a full-time mother? Will the world tell her that she's special just because she is herself? If she makes a mistake at work, will her boss simply smile and hug her – telling her it's ok and that she is special? If you think the answer to these and other questions is a resounding "Yes" then you aren't living in reality. Truth be told, by the time your children are out of your house, they need be able to tie their self-esteem to a constant that is outside of themselves. They need to have an anchor that doesn't move even when the rest of their world might. The only anchor that meets this need is God!

When God looks at your child, what does He see? Does He simply look on the external, or does He focus in on the person she is on the inside? If we look at how he viewed young David just before his anointing as king of Israel, then you and I had better teach our children that the entire exterior is simply that – outside of them. Their real worth is seen when God looks at them from the inside.

As Christian parents, we understand that when we can begin to see ourselves as God sees us, we will be more stable ourselves. Why is it then that we don't take the same approach when advising our children about everyday life? Why do we allow the latest self-help book or TV talk show to advise us on what is best for our children? I am not suggesting those

GAME PLAN

books and TV talk show host aren't studied, or that they never have any good ideas. What I am asking you to consider is how often you turn to those outlets instead of turning to the Bible – God's only inspired Word – when it comes to figuring out how to develop a healthy self-esteem within your children.

As a way to demonstrate, please consider some of the more popular "common sense" statements that are made towards teens when they are faced with dilemmas.

Dilemma 1:
Worried about how to act in a social situation?

Answer: *Just be yourself.*

Dilemma 2:
Concerned about your performance?

Answer: *Believe in yourself.*

Dilemma 3:
Should you buy the new pair of shoes or cut your hair?

Answer: *Yes, express yourself.*

Dilemma 4:
Why should you leave an unfulfilling relationship or quit the boring job?

Answer: *You have to respect yourself.*

WHAT DID WE REALY THINK WOULD HAPPEN?

> **Dilemma 5:**
> Confused about the best time to begin a dating/courtship relationship or even, as older teens, when to get married?
>
> **Answer:** *You have to love yourself before you can love someone else.*
>
> **Dilemma 6:**
> Should you express your opinion?
>
> **Answer:** *Yes, stand up for yourself.*

While you might be thinking to yourself, "Some of these are just common sense and are healthy", please consider who is at the center of each and every one of these statements. It's not whether these are good or bad statements; it's about who we are placing at the center of our lives – in each of these answers, the focus is on the individual. I propose to you that by doing this, we not only hurt our children, but we are teaching them anti-Biblical principles.

In Matthew chapter 22, as Jesus was being questioned by the Pharisee lawyer concerning the greatest commandment in the Law, he said,

> *"You shall love the Lord your God with all your heart, and with all your soul, and with all your mind.' This is the great and foremost commandment. The second is like it, 'You shall love your neighbor as yourself.' On these two commandments depend the whole Law and the Prophets." (v. 37-40)*

Here, Jesus explains that every single aspect of the Old Law is directed at first loving God with everything you are. Love of self is only mentioned as secondary to this, and it's in the context of how we should love our neighbors. Jesus says nothing about the individual placing himself as the center of the universe and therefore placing his neighbor at the center of the universe. The fact the first commandment is God-centered ought to tell us the context of the second commandment. It's only when we understand who we are as God's, and we place Him in His rightful place, that we begin to understand loving our neighbor and loving ourselves.

So, returning to the "common sense" advice we so often give, why is it when our children are concerned about their performance in a baseball game or a class at school, we advise them to believe in themselves, placing the entire focus on them? Instead, why don't we simply say, "Son, regardless how well you do, remember that as a Christian, you are to let your light shine and reflect all glory back to God. Whether you do well or not, what matters is that you bring honor and glory to God?"

I can hear some of you now: "But if my son doesn't excel on the field or in the classroom, it might translate into failure in life." Really?! In whose life? Your child will grow up to be just fine even if he doesn't do well on the baseball field. He will find success in time, possibly in another area of interest. However, if you do not instill in your child (and yes, that includes your teen) that their number one focus should always be on God, then that will impact them for eternity. You and I aren't called by God to raise baseball players, business professionals, school teachers, doctors, and lawyers. We are called to raise young people who have a burning desire to follow God in every stage of life. In so doing, we will teach them that their self-esteem is not tied to stuff, appearance, and even success here on this earth. Rather, their self-esteem, their self-worth, their self-perception is tied to their Creator, and He's will not change or move on them.

THE CONSEQUENCES OF PLACING SELF ON THE THRONE:

In a culture that has done everything it can to dethrone God in the area of absolute truth, we don't have to look very far to see the physical consequences. Despite teenagers reporting higher levels of self-esteem today than previous generations, we continue to see an increase in depression amongst teens. How can those with the highest self-esteem show signs of some of the highest levels of depression that we've seen in teens since such research began?

To find a real answer to this question, I elected to look beyond books and third party research. I sat down on two separate occasions with a small group of teens and asked questions pertaining to self-esteem and the topic of teen depression. I relayed the results of other studies to them, particularly as related to teens today having the highest self-esteem alongside the highest levels of depression and asked their opinion of why this was the case. On both occasions, the group of teens concluded that those who participated in the study must have lied to the researchers. Drawing from their own school experience with anonymous surveys, they relayed that teens like to talk after the surveys were completed. Some teens actually bragged about some of their answers, or joked about them. However, their answers pertaining to sexual involvement or alcohol/drug use were not necessarily truthful. The teens might have over exaggerated or not fully disclosed their participation in that activity. Desire to look a certain way in front of their friends drove them to at least give a false report of their behavior.

This then lead me in another direction. If teens today have the highest self-esteem out of any generation, why would they be concerned about bragging to their friends? After all, isn't that a behavior that is seeking acceptance? Wouldn't such behavior demonstrate that an individual is basing his self-esteem on what peers think about him/her? Why would they do that if they already have extremely high self-esteem?

This question is one that echoes in my head every time I see a report about the mental health of today's teens. Teenagers' high self-esteem should be consistently observable. Instead, while in some cases it is demonstrated well, we continue to see signs that this artificially created self-esteem is not all that it was promised to be.

PLASTIC SURGERY

"It's no different than kids getting braces for crooked teeth," said Dr. Sam Rizk, in a recent article.[7] If you're looking at correcting the angle and shape of one's teeth as a cosmetic procedure, then who can argue with him? Simply put, if a teen's reasoning for wanting his teeth fixed is for a straight smile, that is cosmetic; however, if those crooked teeth are causing a painful problem with the jaw alignment or possibly even with chewing food, then that would be a different situation, right? Similarly, plastic surgery to correct a medical problem is one thing, but plastic surgery simply for the purpose of cosmetics is another.

The subject of teens and plastic surgery was not widely discussed 10 or 20 years ago- although plastic surgeries were taking place, they weren't taking place at today's rates. Although plastic surgery on teenagers only encompasses roughly 2 percent of all plastic surgeries, we must pay attention to recent trends, as the number of such procedures has quadrupled just since 1997.

One reason we've seen an increase in this area is because medical technology has improved, making these procedures safer. However, when it comes to plastic surgery on teens, higher safety levels are not the major driving force. While most adults have plastic surgery to stand out from the crowd, the overwhelming majority of plastic surgeries done on teenagers are to help them fit in with their peers.

Typically, teens gain self-esteem and confidence when their physical "problems" are corrected. What are these physical problems? Most commonly, plastic surgery on teenagers is used to correct a misshapen nose, protruding ears, overly large breasts, asymmetrical breasts, and severe acne and scarring. [8] If these surgeries are done because of a medical problem (for example, overly large breasts causing back problems or a misshapen nose causing breathing problems), then it could be argued that the reason is legitimate. However, if these and other surgeries are done to

WHAT DID WE REALY THINK WOULD HAPPEN?

correct a "problem" and aid the teen in fitting in or gaining self-esteem, then the question must be asked: in a generation that reports having the highest self-esteem out of any previous, why do today's teens need these procedures to increase it? Is this not a sign of low self-esteem?

BULLYING

The most recent *Ethics of American Youth* survey, conducted by the Josephson Institute of Ethics, included feedback from over 43,000 high school students in America. More than 50 percent of those surveyed indicated that they had bullied someone in the past year, and 47 percent said they had been bullied, teased, or taunted in a very serious way. Because of this issue and the violence that often accompanies it, one out of three respondents said violence was a major problem in their schools, and that one out of four said they do not feel very safe at school.[9] Doesn't sound quite like the America you grew up in, does it?

Warning signs of being a victim of bullying:[10]

- Sudden loss of interest in school and school work.
- Frequently complains of physical ailments such as headaches and stomach aches.
- Begins having unexplained nightmares or experiences troubling going to sleep.
- Comes home appearing depressed, moody, sad or teary eyed without provocation.
- Has scratches, bruises, cuts or scrapes that can't be explained.
- Appears afraid to go to school.
- Sudden loss of appetite with bouts of anxiety.
- Has torn or damaged clothes or missing belongings.
- Has few or no friends.

GAME PLAN

All you have to do is turn on the TV or simply walk through the halls of an empty high school and it's pretty obvious that the subject of bullying has become not just a hot topic for the talking heads on TV, but a very serious issue in America. Names such as Phoebe Prince, a 15-year old from Massachusetts, or Hope Witsell, a 13-year old from Florida, echo the pain caused by this epidemic, even as their memories scream from the grave, "Make them stop!" Parents, sometimes unaware, are shocked to discover just how much suffering their children have been enduring at the hands of their peers, and they don't really know what to do.

When we compound the physical and verbal punishment of bullying with the ability to be technologically connected 24 hours a day, we often find ourselves in unchartered territory. The days of actually having to hold a pen and write a name and number on a bathroom stall are ancient. With at least one computer in nearly every American household, and with 75 percent of teens reporting having a Facebook profile[9], a bullying teen can plaster a message to the entire school- or nearly to the entire world- with the push of a button.

Why would they do it though? Why would one teen bully another? There are as many answers to this question as there are people who are willing to answer it. Answers range from "bullies are born that way" or "they are taught this lack of compassion" to "someone must be bullying them at home" or "they don't know how to handle their anger". However, at the core lies an individual's desire to feel better about himself.

Friends, may I remind you that we aren't talking about just one out of ten teens who have been bullied or have bullied someone else. Roughly one out of every two has been bullied, with the same ratio having bullied other people. Granted, there are probably some traits picked up in the home that would lead teenagers to view this as an appropriate way to behave, but these numbers reveal a much larger problem with our society as a whole. For some reason, our teens feel a need to push others down. While those reasons may be different for each child, at the core of the matter is a desire to feel empowered, elevated, and improved at someone else's expense. That's not a sign of high self-esteem! Why does a generation that supposedly has such high self-esteem need to push others down in order to feel better about themselves? It doesn't make sense, does it?

SUICIDE

Did you know that, according to the Center for Disease Control and Prevention, suicide is the third leading cause of death amongst teens every year? This probably doesn't surprise many of you, as it seems almost daily we hear of another teen who decided this was the only way out of life's struggles. What should sadden us, as parents and concerned adults, is the fact that for every suicide completed, there are numerous attempts made (possibly as high as 25 attempts for every one completed) that were "unsuccessful". In any given year, roughly 150,000 teenagers are treated at hospitals for self-inflicted wounds.[11]

A nationwide survey of youth in grades 9-12 in both private and public schools showed that 15 percent of respondents had seriously considered committing suicide.[12] That translates into almost one out of every six of teens having not just considered it, but put serious thought into it. In the same study, 11 percent of the teens surveyed had gone as far to develop a plan. One out of ten had planned the method they would use, decided what time they would make the attempt, and whether they would leave a note. Seven percent said they had tried to take their own life within the last year.[13]

With the number of suicides, an increase in self-mutilating behaviors (i.e. cutting, etc.), and the numerous reports of teens cutting oxygen to the brain as a way to achieve an artificial high, we must again ask the question – "why?" As a society, we have done everything we can think of to promote healthy self-perspective in young people. A positive self-esteem was our goal, and through our "think-tanks" we tried. But rates of depression, bullying, and suicide continue to skyrocket when, all things considered, and if human logic and reasoning is correct, these figures should be decreasing.

BACK TO JUDGES

Reflecting on the cultural push America developed during the 60s and 70s of elevating the individual self, I can't help but wonder if they thought about the possible consequences years down the road. What sounded good then, and what was basically a movement away from God and toward humanism, surely didn't come without a price. As Dr. Twenge observed,

> "Our growing tendency to put the self first leads to unparalleled freedom, but it also created an enormous amount of pressure on us to stand alone."[13]

This concept of standing alone is shown to be in direct conflict with the will of God; we can read this repeatedly in Scripture:

> "Trust in the LORD with all your heart
>   And do not lean on your own understanding.
> In all your ways acknowledge Him,
>   And He will make your paths straight".
>   (Proverbs 3:5-6)
>
> "I know, O LORD, that a man's way is not in himself,
>   Nor is it in a man who walks to direct his steps."
>   (Jeremiah 10:23)
>
> "Many plans are in a man's heart,
>   But the counsel of the LORD will stand."
>   (Proverbs 19:21)

WHAT DID WE REALY THINK WOULD HAPPEN?

When you consider the New Testament, and the teaching pertaining to one's salvation, there is never a positive slant put on the concept of trusting in oneself. When the Bible teaches about obedience, it's always obedience that is directed towards God. The very hope of heaven that we are given is based not upon standing alone, but rather standing in the grace of God. Without Him, we are lost like sheep straying.

The cultural mindset of today truly stands on the opposite side of the battlefield as God, similar to the children of Israel's mindset as displayed in Judges chapters 1 and 2, and as discussed earlier. When the Israelites decided to elevate the individual through their own logic, the consequences were both spiritual and physical. Friends, in our society, we are doing the exact same thing. We have elevated the individual as authority and have placed God on the back burner. That's not to say we aren't attending a worship service somewhere on Sunday morning, but since when did that fully encompass the definition of a true follower of God? A dog can be trained to sit in a pew on a Sunday morning. That doesn't make the dog a Christian.

In John chapter 14, Jesus said,

> **6** *I am the way, and the truth, and the life; no one comes to the Father but through Me.*

Only when we as individuals and as a collective society remember this simple fact can we expect to see positive change. Until we reach that point, America had better brace ourselves for what happens to a nation- and thereby to the individuals within that nation- that doesn't recognize who should be sitting on the throne. As long as we continue to let the individual rule through the advancement of humanism, what is considered horrible today will be commonplace and accepted tomorrow. If you don't believe me, think back about 30 years in our nation's history and ask yourself if this is not true today.

GAME PLAN

CHALK TALK: WHAT'S THE GAME PLAN?

1) Place God's Word as authority in your home, and make sure your teenagers know it.

If all they see is that the Bible is to be picked up on Sunday and Wednesday, your teens will not miraculously catch the idea that the Word of God is valuable and should be in every aspect of their life. As parents, we have the responsibility to not only verbally tell them that God sits on the throne, but we must show them in that we value His Word. Read the Bible with your children. Pray with them. As you make decisions in life, go to the Bible first for guidance, and help your children do the same.

2) Instill in your teen a healthy self-esteem that is tied to God, not to this earth.

The best teacher your teens have is you. When they consider where you gain your self-worth, what do they see? When they hear you talk, what do they hear? Reaffirm God's love in their life on a regular basis. As teenagers, it is tough at times to see love when everything is spinning because of the rush of hormones and the changes that are taking place. Create an environment where they want to talk with you. The only way to accomplish that is to invest in them, and let them know you truly care what they have to say. It's during those moments you will have the opportunity to remind them "aren't you glad God doesn't base your value on the same things as your peers?" and "I'm so glad we serve a God who's not going to leave us for someone else." It

WHAT DID WE REALY THINK WOULD HAPPEN?

might feel strange at first, but I encourage you to continually remind them of the true source of their worth.

CHILDREN ARE BEING SACRIFICED BECAUSE THEY INCONVENIENCE THE PLANS OF THEIR MOTHERS AND FATHERS.

CHAPTER 5

AGENDAS ATTACKING AMERICA
PART 1

Chris was a teenager when we were first introduced. He was very interested in coming to Bible classes and youth outings, although I truly believe at first his motivation was more fueled by the fact that he would get to spend some time with a young lady in the youth group. Over the years, he became a mainstay. If there were an event or a study, even if the young lady he was interested in wasn't there, Chris would show up and participate with an eagerness to learn. Before he graduated from high school, Chris decided to cast his burdens upon Jesus and obey the Gospel. He was even more on fire and enthused to live his life for God, and then he graduated.

I left the youth and family work at that particular congregation, and we lost contact with each other. Then, as happens with many today, Facebook allowed us to get back in touch. While it was nice to talk with Chris and catch up, it became evident that there had been some changes in his life since going off to college. These changes were very evident in his pictures, as he posed with his girlfriend in certain situations that would frankly be disgraceful regardless of who you were or your culture. He and I later spoke in person, and he told me he was no longer attending any particular congregation. Chris had become a statistic like all too many of our youth today.

GAME PLAN

Chris represents something that is very serious and is a reason why I am very passionate about young people and the context of current culture. Today in America, we are losing far too many of our teenagers when they graduate from high school. They revoke their relationship with Jesus and the question has to be asked, "Why"? While there could be many answers to that question, one common denominator is the vastly different culture we live in today.

To illustrate this, I want you to visualize a scene in the late 1700s or early 1800s. Where do you see the father in this scene? Chances are he's around the house plowing with the oxen or doing some type of farming. Maybe he has a job in the local town, but even then, he has to take care of the homestead. Where is the son? In that culture a son, even as young as five years old, would be out in the field with his father. He might be picking up rocks and throwing them out of the way so they could plant crops, or following his father as he builds a barn or mends fences. You would rarely find him sitting around while the father was working. In order to eat, the family had to work.

Where is the mother? The mother typically would be in the house or around the house doing some sort of cleaning or cooking. But here is the most important thing I want you to think about: where is the daughter in this picture? Just as the son was right there with the father, the daughter was right there with her mother, following and learning how to become a grown woman and do the things that her mother was doing.

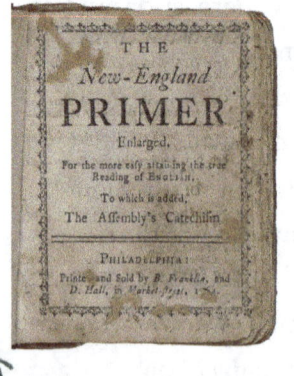

It was truly a different time period. One where if you were to walk thru a community that had a school, you would notice that one of the most prominent textbooks used at the time, the *New England Primer*, contained Scripture that young people would use as they were learning to read and write. Their morals and values were being shaped and molded even as they began to understand more and more of what they were reading.

AGENDAS ATTACKING AMERICA PART 1

It was a time when we had individuals like George Washington who would say,

"It is impossible to rightly govern without God and the Bible."

Or Patrick Henry who said,

"It cannot be emphasized too strongly or too often that this great nation was founded not by religionists but by Christians and not on religions but on the Gospel of Jesus Christ."

Or how about Thomas Jefferson, who is cited as making the statement that became a precedent for the separation of Church and State? While many claim he was either an agnostic or an atheist, it was Jefferson who would state,

"Can the liberties of a nation be thought secure when we have removed their only firm basis- a conviction in the minds of the people that these liberties are of the gift of God? That they are not to be violated but with His wrath? Indeed, I tremble for my country when I reflect that God is just; that His justice cannot sleep forever."

Does this sound like the words of a man who thought God didn't exist or that He isn't active in the world? Of course not! However, many individuals today are twisting history and teaching that a large number of our nation's founding fathers were atheists or agnostics. Granted, while a few didn't believe in the existence and work of God, the majority absolutely did.

These men made bold statements about their belief in God and about the wrath of God that would fall upon a culture that turned their eyes away from Him and their backs to Him. They knew, without Americans looking to God's Word for guidance and direction, that America would be quickly lost. It truly was a different time and culture.

By Def·i·ni·tion

re·vi·sion·ist —n
a person attempting to reevaluate and restate the past based on newly acquired standards.

GAME PLAN

THE LAND OF CANAAN: THE CULTURE AND PEOPLE

Next, I want you to go on a journey with me in Genesis chapter 12, where we notice something about a man we simply know as Abram. Beginning with verse 1, we read,

> *1 Now the LORD said to Abram,*
>   *"Go forth from your country,*
>   *And from your relatives*
>   *And from your father's house,*
>   *To the land which I will show you;*
> *2 And I will make you a great nation,*
>   *And I will bless you,*
>   *And make your name great;*
>   *And so you shall be a blessing;*
> *3 And I will bless those who bless you,*
>   *And the one who curses you I will curse,*
>   *And in you all the families of the earth*
>   *will be blessed." (Genesis 2: 1-3)*

When we look at the call of Abram, we see he is commanded to leave three aspects of his life behind – country, relatives, and father's house. For us today, this may not be as significant. However, when we consider the time period, this is a tall order. He's called to leave all human security behind him and walk forward in an unfamiliar direction, faithfully trusting in God to lead him into the Promised Land of Canaan. While we don't learn much about this Promised Land in Genesis chapter 12, the window is opened more in Exodus chapter 3 at the call of Moses.

It is here we read of God speaking to Moses from the bush on the mountain of Horeb:

> 7 ..."I have surely seen the affliction of My people who are in Egypt, and have given heed to their cry because of their taskmasters, for I am aware of their sufferings.
>
> 8 "So I have come down to deliver them from the power of the Egyptians, and to bring them up from that land to a good and spacious land, to a land flowing with milk and honey, to the place of the Canaanite and the Hittite and the Amorite and the Perizzite and the Hivite and the Jebusite." (Exodus 3: 7-8)

While this land is promised by God in Genesis chapter 12, Exodus 3 describes it as a land that is "good and spacious" and "flowing with milk and honey", pointing to how blessed the inhabitants of the land would be. However, we also learn the land is already claimed by the Canaanites, Hittites, Amorites, Perizzites, Hivites, and Jebusites. Turning our attention to Leviticus chapter 18, we begin to see just exactly the types of things these groups are doing in Canaan, this Promised Land that God has given to the nation of Israel to live in prosperously:

> 20 'You shall not have intercourse with your neighbor's wife, to be defiled with her.
>
> 21 'You shall not give any of your offspring to offer them to Molech, nor shall you profane the name of your God; I am the LORD.
>
> 22 'You shall not lie with a male as one lies with a female; it is an abomination.
>
> 23 'Also you shall not have intercourse with any animal to be defiled with it, nor shall any woman stand before an animal to mate with it; it is a perversion.
>
> 24 'Do not defile yourselves by any of these things; for by all these the nations which I am casting out before you have become defiled.

GAME PLAN

> **25** 'For the land has become defiled, therefore I have brought its punishment upon it, so the land has spewed out its inhabitants.
>
> **26** 'But as for you, you are to keep My statutes and My judgments and shall not do any of these abominations, neither the native, nor the alien who sojourns among you *(Leviticus 18: 20-26)*

Along with the very long list of sexual sins present in the land, there is also a religious dilemma which the Israelites will face. In verse 21, the god Molech and the practices of child sacrifice are addressed, indicating a major practice of the people who were living in the land at the time. This false god, Molech, is believed to have been represented as a large image with the belly carved out of it and a fire blazing inside. In order to worship this god, parents would bring their infant children to a priest and he would throw the child into the belly of fire. As the child would burn alive, drummers would play at the base so as to drown out the cries of the child. This was all in the name of worship.

When we read of this and the fact that God was sending His select children into this land filled with child sacrifice, idol worship, and all types of sexual immorality, one can't help but ask, "What type of society would do this?" Why did God not simply send His people to another land that was "good and spacious" and "flowing with milk and honey" but that didn't contain this immoral people?

While these questions are fair, the answer is best understood in looking at the nature of God… the very nature that follows through on promises made. When God created this land and selected it for the children of Israel, His plan was set in motion. When He promised this land to Abram in Genesis chapter 12, the plan had been communicated. When Moses was called, the promise was reaffirmed. Our God is faithful and keeps His promises.

AGENDAS ATTACKING AMERICA PART 1

> *Know therefore that the LORD your God, He is God, the faithful God, who keeps His covenant and His lovingkindness to a thousandth generation with those who love Him and keep His commandments; (Deuteronomy 7:9)*
>
> *God is faithful, through whom you were called into fellowship with His Son, Jesus Christ our Lord. (1 Corinthians 1: 9)*
>
> *Let us hold fast the confession of our hope without wavering, for He who promised is faithful; (Hebrews 10: 23)*

When reflecting on the sin and immorality saturating the people of the land of Canaan, one might start to consider whether we struggle with the same issues the Canaanites struggled with, and what is the answer for God's children today. I propose to you that yes, we do struggle with the exact same immorality, including idol worship; however, the god we worship is the god of self. We love to have our ideas wrapped around our own needs, and our own wants, and our own desires. Our society teaches children they can become anything they want to, even if it means running over people to get there. We truly have become a very self-centered society. With this self-centeredness as a major driving force, agenda machines have taken full advantage. Child sacrifice was happening in the land of Canaan as a form of worship. This same issue plaques America today, but we hide it under a different name and what has become a political issue.

GAME PLAN

THE ABORTION AGENDA

As we consider the concept of abortion and the whole debate of when life begins, we first need to realize that this issue has become so politicized that it's no longer about whether the child should be considered a human being and thus have the protection granted to all Americans by the Constitution. It was Supreme Court Justice Harry Blackmun, when writing the majority decision in *Roe v. Wade* who stated,

Supreme Court Justice Harry Blackmun

"We need not resolve the difficult question of when life begins. When those trained in the respective disciplines of medicine, philosophy and theology are unable to arrive at any consensus, the judiciary, at this point in the development of man's knowledge, is not in a position to speculate as to the answer."[1]

There are plenty of people, some well-studied and others simply opinionated, who would disagree as to when life begins. However, unlike Justice Blackman, I suggest that answering that question is crucial in understanding and confronting the abortion agenda.

THROUGH THE LENS OF SCIENCE

It is a well-known fact that our bodies operate through systems such as the circulatory system, respiratory system, and digestive system, etc. Each of these systems is comprised of organs, which are made of tissues. These tissues, when broken down to their smallest level, are made up of cells. Each cell contains various components that when functioning as a unit, operate in a healthy manner, thereby allowing the body to function well. Part of the cell's healthy function is in its ability to metabolize and thus divide, making new cells. If the cell ever stops metabolizing, it will die. If a

AGENDAS ATTACKING AMERICA PART I

group of cells die, the tissue dies. Ultimately, it becomes a domino effect: if enough of the same tissues die, the organ is compromised or dies and thus the system begins to suffer. If you have enough cells that die, the human dies and life is gone. It's a chain, connected just as God designed; therefore, it is completely necessary to have cellular metabolism taking place in order to have life.

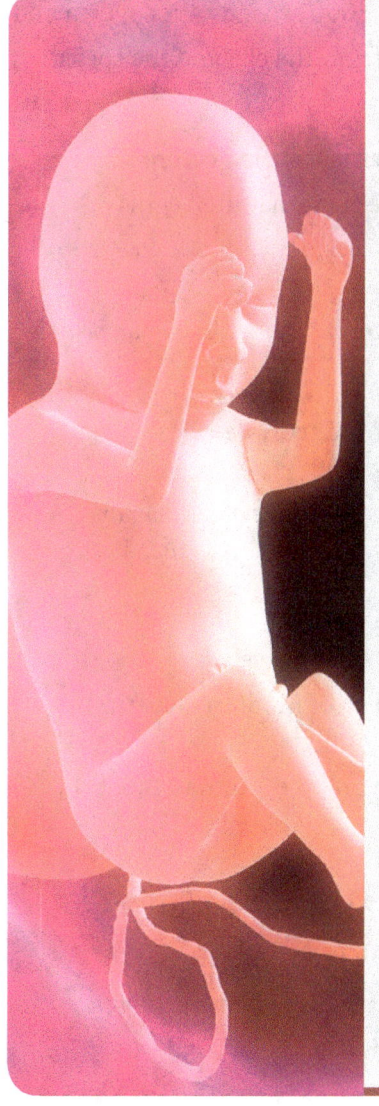

Development of an Unborn Baby:[2]

Day 1 - Fertilization: all human chromosomes present; unique human life begins

Day 6 – Implantation in the uterus

Day 22 - Heart begins to beat with the child's own blood

Week 5 - Eyes, legs, hands begin to develop

Week 6 - Brain waves are noticeable; mouth and lips begin to develop

Week 7 – Eyelids and toes form; nose is distinct, baby kicking and swimming

Week 8 - every organ is in place; bones and fingerprints begin to form

Weeks 9 and 10 - Teeth begin to form, fingernails develop; baby can turn head and frown

Continued on next page

GAME PLAN

> **Week 11** - Baby can grasp objects placed in hand
>
> **Week 17** - Baby can have dream (REM) sleep
>
> **Week 20** – Baby can recognize mother's voice

Why the science lesson? Understanding these basic concepts, you are now poised to recognize the significance of the fact that cellular division, and therefore metabolism, occurs in the first 6000 seconds after sperm and an egg unite.[3] Once the genetics are in place from the egg and the sperm, metabolism begins; thus, life is conceived.

In 1981, a group of physicians and geneticists testified before the Senate Judiciary Committee, with all in agreement that life begins upon conception.

> *"The exact moment of the beginning of personhood and of the human body is at the moment of conception."*
>
> – Dr. McCarthy de Mere

> *"To accept the fact that after fertilization has taken place a new human has come into being is no longer a matter of taste or opinion…it is plain experimental evidence."*
>
> – Dr. Jerome Lejeune
> (Father of Modern Genetics)

The Official Senate report on Senate Bill 158, the "Human Life Bill," summarized the issue this way:

> *Physicians, biologists, and other scientists agree that conception marks the beginning of the life of a human being—a being that is alive and is a member of the human species. There is overwhelming agreement on this point in countless medical, biological, and scientific writings.*[4]

The issue of when life begins, from a scientific standpoint, is truly no longer up for debate. Tests have been conducted and the results duplicated time after time. However, as mentioned earlier, this is not simply a scientific issue. "Big money" and liberal-minded individuals have created a very political side of the agenda. These people do not respect the life of the child, and most importantly, they do not respect what God's Word has to say on the issue.

THROUGH THE LENS OF THE BIBLE

It is significant to notice from a Biblical perspective that God looks at the child inside of the mother's womb in the same light as an infant. This is demonstrated when reading and considering the original language pertaining to the English word "baby" as seen in Luke chapters 1 and 2.

> *41 When Elizabeth heard Mary's greeting, the baby leaped in her womb; and Elizabeth was filled with the Holy Spirit. (Luke 1:41)*
>
> *44 For behold, when the sound of your greeting reached my ears, the baby leaped in my womb for joy. (Luke 1:44)*
>
> *12 This will be a sign for you: you will find a baby wrapped in cloths and lying in a manger. (Luke 2:12)*
>
> *16 So they came in a hurry and found their way to Mary and Joseph, and the baby as He lay in the manger. (Luke 2:16)*

GAME PLAN

In these passages, we see the word "baby" used to refer to children at different stages. In chapter one, the reference is to a child inside the mother's womb; however, in chapter two, the child being spoken of is outside the mother's womb. The significance lies in the fact that the original language, the Greek, uses the exact same word, brephos, to describe both children. There were other words the Holy Spirit could have inspired Luke to use when referring to the child outside the mother's womb, such as teknon (the generic word for "child") or even teknion, (the word often used for "small child"). However, by purpose, the Holy Spirit inspired Luke to use the word brephos to describe the children at the different stages. Thus the one inside the womb is considered just as much a child as the one outside the womb. [5]

This is demonstrated even further when one considers the Old Testament teaching commonly known as the *lex talionis* or the *law of retaliation* as it pertained to men fighting around a pregnant woman.

> **22** *If men struggle with each other and strike a woman with child so that she gives birth prematurely, yet there is no injury, he shall surely be fined as the woman's husband may demand of him, and he shall pay as the judges decide.* **23** *But if there is any further injury, then you shall appoint as a penalty life for life,* **24** *eye for eye, tooth for tooth, hand for hand, foot for foot,* **25** *burn for burn, wound for wound, bruise for bruise. (Exodus 21: 22-25)*

In a very clear way, Moses communicates the value of protecting a pregnant woman and her child. If the woman were to be injured or killed, then there would be equal payment made. However, the indication of this passage also merits the same respect be given to her child. If the child is injured or is delivered prematurely and dies, then a penalty was ordered by God which superseded any recourse from the child's father or judges. The penalty was to be Life for Life.

If the child inside the mother's womb is not a living human life, why would a man need to pay with his own life? Furthermore, when considering the New Testament, if the child inside the mother's womb is not a living human life, why would the Holy Spirit inspire Luke to use a word that carries of a meaning as such? The answer, from a Biblical perspective is clear: the baby in the womb is a human being and valuable to God, as He shapes and forms each child.

> **13** *For You formed my inward parts; You wove me in my mother's womb. (Psalm 139: 13)*

THROUGH THE LENS OF LOGIC

The argument has been made on numerous occasions that since the "unborn child" cannot live outside of the mother's womb, the child is not granted the same constitutionally protected rights as every other human being in America. Thus, people conclude that the woman has a right to control her body and to choose whether to terminate a pregnancy. To understand the logical fallacy in this argument, I would like for us to consider the following situation.

Picture in your mind a person who has been put on life support - maybe an older man who had a stroke or possibly a teenager just learning to drive, who looks down at his cell phone, only to hit an oncoming car head-on. Once the person arrives at the hospital, doctors and nurses rush to insert the necessary tubes to stabilize the patient, and more to sustain him as he is placed in the Intensive Care Unit.

Now, picture yourself standing in the open doorway of his room. As you observe the breathing machine working, and you see the feeding tube running out from under the sheet, can you look at this person and claim he is not a human being? We might say that their quality of life has been seriously diminished; however, doctors and nurses would not work so hard to bring about healing if the person lying in the bed was not a human being. It is illogical to conclude that because the person has to have life support for a time, that they are not a human being. If you stop the life support before his body is ready to sustain life on its own again, the patient will die. However, nearly all of us have known someone who had to be on life support for a time; then, once their body had healed enough, the machines were removed. Today, they are just as alive as you and I.

With the same logic, now consider a child who is hooked up to a life support system through the mother's umbilical cord. He or she receives nutrition and oxygen through the blood needed to sustain life. If you cut the life support of that child before she is ready to sustain life on her own, she will die just like the person in our scenario above. This fact doesn't make the child anything less than a human being. The same logic holds true for the adult, teen, and child.

THE REAL ISSUE:

In America, we are quite inconsistent on the issue of when life begins. Consider the case of California's Scott Peterson, who was convicted of killing his wife, Laci, while she was pregnant. Peterson was charged with double homicide, which opens up an obvious question: why was he charged with the killing of a human being if the child was still inside of Laci's womb? Proponents of abortion consider it an American woman's "right" to enter an abortion clinic and kill the baby within her; she isn't going to be charged with any crime. If this is acceptable, then how do we justify saying that a father can't choose to kill the baby as well? That doesn't make sense, does it?

The abortion agenda is not about making sense. It's not about what true science has discovered, what the Bible has to say on the issue, nor about simple logic. Unfortunately, our culture has developed an attitude of "it's all about me". We have become a society of self-absorbed individuals who will do whatever makes us feel good and right. This becomes obvious when you consider that since the Roe v. Wade decision on January 22, 1973, there have been over 50,000,000 children sacrificed to the "god of self".[6] Of those women who have an abortion each year, over half are in their 20s and 19 percent are teenagers.[7]

These babies were sacrificed because they got in the way of our "I am the most important person" philosophy; this is shockingly clear when you consider the reasons American women report as their rationale for having an abortion:

- Feels unready for child/responsibility — **25%**
- Feels she can't afford baby — **23%**
- Other family responsibilities — **19%**
- Relationship problem/single motherhood — **8%**
- Feels she isn't mature enough — **7%**
- Other reasons — **>6.5%**
- Interference with education/career plans — **4%**
- Mother's health — **4%**
- Baby may have health problem — **3%**
- Parents/partner wants abortion — **>1%**
- Rape — **>0.5%**[8]

When 93 percent of the abortions had are reported to be for social reasons, it's time we wake up to the reality that Americans aren't having abortions on the whole because of the sensitive and hard circumstances surrounding rape and incest. Children are being sacrificed because they inconvenience the plans of their mothers and fathers.

We have an ever-increasing epidemic that is being pushed upon us through various educational and media outlets that endorse the concept of sex before marriage as a standard part of growing up. These organizations will often promote the idea that, if a fetus results from your "playtime", you have the right to get rid of "it" because "it" can't feel anything anyway. That's exactly what Abby Johnson, a former employee

GAME PLAN

of Planned Parenthood used to tell young girls as she counseled them on family planning. That all changed on October 26, 2009, when she actually had to assist with an abortion and saw the child moving away from the instrument that was inserted to kill.

Abby Johnson

Abby Johnson: On September 26 (2009), that's when I actually saw an ultrasound-guided abortion procedure. Ultrasound-guided abortions are very uncommon. They are particularly uncommon in large abortion facilities like Planned Parenthood. If we are talking about abortion in terms of safe procedures for the woman, ultrasound-guided procedures are the safest procedure. It is the best type of procedure for the woman. There's less risk of uterine perforation. These big places don't want to do it because it takes more time.

This particular physician who was coming down that day is a private practice abortion physician. He has his own practice out of town and he was coming in to do abortions as a visiting physician that day. In his practice he only does ultrasound-guided abortions. The patient was a little further along in her pregnancy—about 13 weeks—so the doctor decided that on this patient he was going to do an ultrasound-guided procedure. For that procedure he needed an extra person in the room to hold the ultrasound probe, and that was me.

So they called me into the room and told me they would need me to hold the ultrasound probe on her abdomen so that he could see the uterus during the procedure. That was to be my job during the procedure. So we had everything in place, and I saw on the screen a thirteen-week baby. You know at thirteen weeks—even at ten weeks— what you see on the ultrasound is a fully formed baby with arms and legs. Everything is fully formed. If you can get a good profile view, you can see all of this.

Well, this was a good profile view. I could see everything from head to foot. And then I saw the probe—called a cannula, that is hooked up to the suction machine—I saw that go into the woman's uterus. And then I saw it jab into the side of the baby. Then, in just a few seconds, I saw the baby begin to react to that jabbing. I saw the baby's arms and legs begin to move. The baby was trying to get away from the probe.

Focus Press: Wow. I have to ask this because I'm sitting here trying to imagine it for myself: What were you going through internally at that point?

Abby Johnson: Well, I couldn't believe what I was looking at. I felt sick to my stomach. I realized what I was about to look at and I realized what I was about to see. And that's when they turned on the suction. A baby at that age has a perfectly formed backbone. The last thing I saw was the backbone going through the cannula on the ultrasound screen. I'll never forget what it looked like on the screen. You know how they say with a train wreck you don't want to watch but you can't stop looking at it? That's what it was like for me. I didn't want to look at it, but I couldn't stop looking at the screen. When I saw that baby moving, it was like he was waking up and then trying to get away from the cannula.

I immediately thought of all the women I had lied to. You get a lot of questions in the room. As a counselor in the room with women, they ask you questions before they go back for their abortion procedure. One of the things they ask you frequently is, "Is my baby going to feel this?" Every time I had told them no. Because I really didn't think the baby would feel it. **Planned Parenthood had told me they wouldn't feel it, so I told them no.** I immediately thought about all the women I had lied to. I was thinking to myself, "What if I had told them the truth?

GAME PLAN

What if I had known the truth— would I still be here at this job? Would those women have chosen an abortion?" What kind of difference would it have made if we had all known the truth? **Why are they trying to hide this?"**

(You can read the entire interview in the appendix.)

The agenda surrounding abortion, while it might seem like an old issue, is widely pervasive in today's culture. Teenagers today don't remember what America was like before Roe v. Wade; they weren't alive then. Politicians discuss and debate the subject. News channels are quick to report on it. High profile individuals are ready to endorse it. Some schools encourage it. If we're not careful, our young people, even those who are Christians, are going to be so saturated with information given by those driving the agenda that confusion and uncertainty will surface even more than it already has.

CHALK TALK: WHAT'S THE GAME PLAN?

1) Know what you're up against!

It's one thing to know what abortion is; it's altogether different to understand how the subject of abortion or "family planning" is being communicated to your child or the young people with whom you work. While the majority of states in America still require some form of communication with the parents before a child can have abortion, the real problem is occurring before the abortion is even considered. It's occurring through the indoctrination of our young people to believe that sex before marriage is part of life and that contraceptives are the way to go. What's being taught in the health books your children study? What is the policy your student is subject to when sexuality is taught in her local school? You must know what you're up against.

AGENDAS ATTACKING AMERICA PART 1

2) Talk with your children about the sanctity of life as demonstrated in the Bible and even about the dangers of premarital sex.

It's important to express that life is special and babies should not be aborted; however, your child will very likely be given all kinds of scientific reasons why abortions should be allowed. The heart-strings will be pulled, and confusion will result. As parents, God has placed on our shoulders the responsibility to train our children in His ways as revealed in the Bible. How can we teach them if we don't know ourselves? We know abortions shouldn't happen, but why? First study and be grounded yourself, then teach and ground your children in the strong truth of the Word of God as it pertains to sexuality and children. This is not a "one-and-done" conversation. It must be a subject you dare address on a regular basis as your child is growing. We cannot remain silent, hoping we never have to address the issue. If we choose not to speak to our children, then they will only hear one side of the issue. Your love must drive you to speak straight with them.

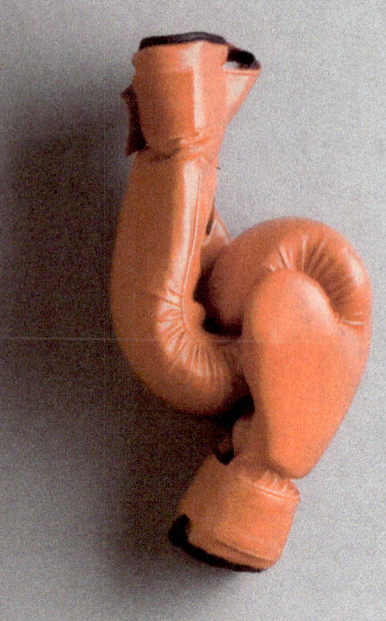

IT'S A FOREGONE CONCLUSION THAT THE AMERICAN VIEWPOINT ON HOMOSEXUALITY HAS CHANGED DRASTICALLY OVER THE YEARS.

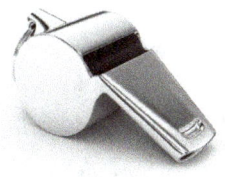

CHAPTER 6

AGENDAS ATTACKING AMERICA
PART 2

THE HOMOSEXUAL AGENDA

We've discussed how the pagan people in the land of Canaan were performing child sacrifice. Along with this, they were also participating in the act of homosexuality. And our society today seems to be following them in this regard as well, heading down the same pathway with an ever-increasing acceptance of the homosexual lifestyle. This was seen very clearly in the May 26, 2010 Gallup Poll: for the first time, the majority of those polled (52 percent) said that homosexual relationships were morally acceptable. [1] While this study begs the question of what standards are being used to measure morality, let's first consider how we came to this way of thinking in America.

It's a foregone conclusion that the American viewpoint on homosexuality has changed drastically over the years. In looking back through our founding fathers' documents, it is very clear that homosexuality was not accepted and tolerated. Thomas Jefferson's *Notes on the State of Virginia: Query XIII* outlined that sodomy was to be punished

GAME PLAN

by dismemberment. Sodomy was punishable by death in colonies such as Connecticut, New York, Vermont, and South Carolina. Even as late as 1986, in response to the *Bowers v. Hardwick* case, which challenging the sodomy laws of the state of Georgia, the U.S. Supreme Court stated,

> *"Proscriptions against that conduct have ancient roots…Sodomy was a criminal offense at common law and was forbidden by the laws of the original 13 States when they ratified the Bill of Rights."*[2]

With this ruling, the U.S. Supreme Court testified to the sentiment of colonial America, upheld the rights of the individual states to choose their own laws pertaining to sodomy, and advocated the constitutionality of sodomy laws at that time. Protests against homosexuality, including the June 1969 riots at the controversial dance club known as the Stonewall Inn, in New York's Greenwich Village, demonstrated that the moral standard in America was still at a level where homosexuality was not accepted.

Through the 1970s, the homosexual agenda picked up steam, marked by the American Psychiatric Association's decision in 1973 to remove homosexuality from their official list of mental disorders. From this era into the 1980s, the newly recognized AIDS epidemic thrust the subject of homosexuality further into the political lime-light, as "fearful compassion" surfaced. Many Americans, worried about contracting the AIDS virus, shunned active homosexuals, realizing this community had a higher rate of contracting the AIDS virus due to their high number of sexual partners, demonstrated by a 1978 study in which most homosexual men reported having at least 50 partners in their lifetime.[3] America watched as homosexuals suffered a scary death at the hands of this disease; gradually, too, we became very aware of the disease's ability to claim the lives of non-homosexuals, through the transmission of other bodily fluids. This was the case with tennis legend Arthur Ashe, who contracted the virus through a blood transfusion.

CRACK IN THE FOUNDATION

Timeline for Homosexuality in America:

1962 Illinois becomes the first state to decriminalize homosexual acts between consenting adults

1973 The American Psychiatric Association removes "homosexuality" from it's list of mental disorders

1993 "Don't Ask Don't Tell" is instituted in the U.S. military

2000 Vermont becomes the first state to recognize civil unions for homosexual couples

2004 Same-sex marriages become legal in Massachusetts.

2005 Civil unions become legal in Connecticut.

2006 Civil unions become legal in New Jersey.

2007 The House of Representatives approves a bill ensuring equal rights in the workplace for gay men, lesbians, and bisexuals.

2008 The state of Oregon passes a law that allows same-sex couples to register as domestic partners allowing them some spousal rights of married couples.

2008 The Supreme Court of Connecticut rules that same-sex couples have the right to marry, making this the second state to do so.

2009 The Iowa Supreme Court rejects a state law banning same-sex marriage.

2009 New Hampshire is the sixth state in the nation to allow same-sex marriage.

2010 Congress approves a law that legalizes same-sex marriage in the District of Columbia.

2010 Chief U.S. District Judge Vaughn Walker ruled that Proposition 8, the 2008 referendum that banned same-sex marriage in California, violates the 14th Amendment's equal protection clause.

2010 "Don't Ask, Don't Tell" is repealed.

GAME PLAN

It was in this cultural environment that those who wanted to push the advancement of the homosexual agenda decided to harness the compassion of America. They knew if handled correctly, homosexuals suffering from AIDS could be painted as victims, further changing the way Americans thought about this sinful behavior.

THE WAR CONFERENCE OF 1988

In 1988 a conference held in Warrington, Virginia, brought together 175 leading activists from various homosexual groups from across the nation, that they might determine how to change America's view of homosexuality. Shortly after, a book was written mapping out their plan of attack, entitled *After the Ball: How America Will Conquer Its Fear and Hatred of Gays in the 90's*.[4] The authors, Marshal Kirk and Hunter Madsen, were both from very prestigious schools, MIT and Harvard, and were well studied in areas such as neuropsychiatry and social marketing. With these tools in their holsters, they would explain how the time was right to take advantage of the AIDS epidemic. They wrote, "As cynical as it may seem, AIDS gives us a chance, however brief, to establish ourselves as a victimized minority legitimately deserving of America's special protection and care." When addressing the issue of the fear and concern they wrote, "How can we maximize the sympathy and minimize the fear? How, given the horrid hand that AIDS has dealt us, can we best play it?"[5] It is clear that their agenda was to ride the AIDS wave as a way of advancing their cause. They would desensitize Americans by advancing the battle lines with weapons of propaganda, advertising, and psychology.

One of their tactics was simply changing the lexicon. By moving the word for this sinful activity away from "homosexual" to the culturally accepted and positive word "gay", they could promote a different understanding and solicit a different emotional response from the hearer. After all, the word "gay" once meant "happy". Controlling the language of the debate, they knew their likelihood of winning increased significantly.

AGENDAS ATTACKING AMERICA PART 2

They also decided that, instead of making the debate over the moral issue, they would make it into an element of civil rights, thus standing on the coat tails of individuals who had to fight for the right to drink out of certain water fountains or to sit at certain places on the bus. In doing so, they would frame the boundaries of the debate around the issue of human rights. It could then be argued that in not accepting their lifestyle, America was denying the homosexual community basic freedoms granted to them as citizens.

> **By Defi·ni·tion**
>
> **1950s' understanding:**
> **gay** —adj
> having or showing a merry, lively mood
>
> **Current understanding:**
> **gay** —adj
> homosexual

The results of this purposed attack are evident today. The media no longer references the morality or the consequences of homosexuality; they instead discuss the matter of "gay rights". When you watch television shows, many contain a homosexual element, which is treated as mainstream and accepted. Truth be told, if the show contains characters who don't accept this lifestyle, they are portrayed as old-fashioned, or intolerant homophobes. Commercials today, both on television and in print ads, use homosexuality as the current and "hip" tactic to attract customers and make a statement about their company policies of acceptance and tolerance.

We live in a society today where, politically speaking, the issue of health benefits, retirement benefits, adoption benefits, and numerous other subjects historically reserved for a husband and wife, are now being considered for homosexual relationships. Even the very definition of "marriage" has been challenged in many states. In November 2008, citizens of California voted to pass Proposition 8 as an amendment to the state constitution, which

ProtectMarriage.com

defined marriage as being between one man and one woman.[6] This historical vote created a chasm not only in California, but also across America; the passion people had for the topic was evidenced in the amount of money raised both for and against the proposition ($38.7 million and $44.1 million, respectively).[7] It was the most funded debate and vote outside of the presidential contest that our nation has ever experienced. Although the people of California spoke through the ballot box in 2008, on August 4, 2010, Proposition 8 was ruled to be unconstitutional by Federal Judge Vaughn R. Walker, silencing the votes of Californians at the federal level, and resulting in further division.

Looking at the width and breadth of this debate, it's sometimes difficult to narrow our focus and observe just exactly how this agenda is playing out in regard to our children. Clearly, as our children watch the television shows and read the magazines, advertisements and stories attempt to teach them certain mindsets. However, our society has another tactic for changing the way the next generation views the issue of homosexuality, one that Madsen and Kirk wrote about in *After the Ball*:

> "When you're very different, and people hate you for it, this is what you do: first you get your foot in the door, by being as similar as possible; then, and only then – when your one little difference is finally accepted – can you start dragging in your other peculiarities, one by one. You hammer in the wedge narrow end first. As the saying goes, allow the camel's nose beneath your tent, and his whole body will soon follow."[8]

THE ASSAULT ON CHILDREN

Unfortunately, there is a hammer and a wedge being used today, and the major group that is yielding it when it comes to our children is GLESN (Gay, Lesbian, and Straight Education Alliance). This is the organization responsible for The Day of Silence protest, which directs students to not speak for an entire day in protest of the way homosexual and bisexual students are treated. GLESN also sponsors the campaign ThinkB4YouSpeak, aimed at cutting down on the number of hurtful expressions used by many teens (i.e. "That's so gay!"). At first impression, both of which sound like innocent and good campaigns. After all, every parent would love for the amount of harsh words and bullying to be cut down. We mourn every time we hear of another teenager taking his or her own life for any reason. GLESN knows this and has decided this will be their major frontal attack. They paint themselves as the protector and defender of all teenagers; however, as the bottom current swells and momentum is gained, their true agenda can be seen in the advancement of Gay-Straight Alliance groups (GSAs) in middle schools and high schools.

School clubs are about as old as the current education model. There are service-oriented clubs such as the Key Club; education-oriented clubs such as the National Honor Society; and spirited clubs such as the Pep Club. If one were to look at an average middle school or high school on any given "club day" you could likely find just about any group with any purpose for meeting - including GSAs, which serve to advance the acceptance of the homosexual lifestyle amongst teenagers.

According to the website for GLESN, there are currently over 4,000 of these groups registered across America.[9] Along with their regular meetings, these groups are encouraged to hang up posters, talk with their fellow students and teachers, as well as host seminars and participate in school fairs that would serve to further their cause, which is tolerance of a lifestyle that is against the Bible. It is through this indoctrination, teenagers are taught that homosexuals are just like any other people and that their one little difference ought to be tolerated. That's the exact approach Madsen and Kirk advocated in order to change America.

Along with this targeted attack on our middle school and high school age children, the very young are not safe anymore. The GLESN website also directs teachers how to teach tolerance to elementary age children; one such method is introducing students as young as age 5 to the reality

GAME PLAN

differences will exist in campaigns such as "We're All Different Alike".[10] With this first strike of the hammer on the wedge, the thought process has been primed for the rest of GLESN's approach, which will eventually include how to have a positive environment in the schools for Lesbians, Gays, Bisexual and Transgender students (LGBT). This façade of being ambassadors for all students quickly deteriorates when you do a little research on their website. However, our elementary age school children, whom most don't care about going on the Internet for much other than playing games, aren't going to research this agenda on their own.

Along with some classrooms in America serving as the medium to advance the homosexual agenda, we also see cute children's books being published and carried in many of our public libraries and even school libraries. Such books include:

> *King and King*, published by Tricycle Press [11]
>
> This children's story focuses in on a single prince and his overbearing mother, a queen who demands it's time the prince marry (I don't know if it is supposed to be deduced from the plot, but there is no mention of the queen's husband in this book). She brings in princesses from all across the world; however, her son has already made it clear "...I've never cared much for princesses." After seeing all the young ladies, the prince finally sees his "love"— the brother who escorted his princess sister to the palace. The two men fall in love, get married, and live happily ever after. The cherry on top is the final illustrated page which shows the two men leaning in to kiss each other with a heart drawn over their lips.

AGENDAS ATTACKING AMERICA PART 2

Molly's Family, published by Farrar Straus Grioux [12]

> This story line sets out to describe how tough children can be on one another, especially if they don't understand family situations. The way the author then handles this situation is to set the scene for an open house in Molly's classroom. She has "Mommy" and "Mama Lu", both of whom are women. When she draws a picture of her family, some of the boys in the class tell her that she can't have two mommies. When Molly goes home that night, "Mommy" and "Mama Lu" explain to her that they had been living together for some time and wanted to have a child to share their love with, so "Mommy" became pregnant with Molly. The two women went before a judge and "Mama Lu" was allowed to adopt Molly, giving Molly two mothers.

Oh The Things Mommies Do! What Could Be Better Than Having Two?, published by Crystal Tompkins [13]

> As the title tells, this book is about the "blessings" having two mommies bring to children's lives. They cook for you, clean you up, care for your wounds, and take you to the zoo. Missing from this book are any pictures of men and any suggestion that men might offer intrinsic value to a child's life. An incredibly striking aspect of this book, outside of the obvious teaching of how wonderful it is to have lesbian mothers, is a page that reads, "They teach you how to follow the rules"; subsequently, the very first rule listed is "Treat others as you want to be treated". While not a direct quote, it sure sounds like the author is appealing to Matthew 7:12 which reads,
>
> *"In everything, therefore, treat people the same way you want them to treat you, for this is the Law and the Prophets."*
>
> Here you have a children's book teaching the benefits of

homosexuality while, at the same time, bringing the authority of the Bible into the "rules" teaching. Ironic and very sad!

ARE HOMOSEXUALS BORN THAT WAY?

In an October 6, 2008 interview with People magazine, American Idol phenomenon Clay Aiken decided to "come clean" on his homosexual lifestyle. As he introduced his son Parker to the world, Aiken said about announcing his homosexuality, "It was the first decision I made as a father. I cannot raise a child to lie or to hide things. I wasn't raised that way, and I'm not going to raise a child to do that."[14] Aiken would go on to say when asked about his hopes for Parker,

> "I want to raise him in an environment that is accepting and allowing him to be happy. I have no idea if he'll be gay or straight. It's not something I'll have anything to do with, or that he'll have anything to do with. It's already probably up inside the code there, you know what I mean?" In making this statement, Aiken chimed in on the long-standing debate over whether or not homosexuals are "born that way" or if their environment influenced them as they grew through childhood, adolescence and into adulthood. His answer –it's "up inside the code there".

Is it really, or is that simply a decoy used by some who want to push the homosexual agenda and legitimize that lifestyle? Advocates for homosexuality argue, if they are born with a genetic predisposition to it, then how can they help it? If there really is a "gay gene" then they are only reacting to how they were made. Will God really eternally punish someone who is merely responding to their genetic make-up, which is ultimately out of their control? There is a lot in our current culture riding on the answer to these questions; let's answer the first by looking at real studies and real evidences.

AGENDAS ATTACKING AMERICA PART 2

In the August 1991 issue of Science, Dr. Simon LeVay, at the time, a scientist with the Salk Institute for Biological Studies in San Diego, CA, reported that his studies had shown a significant difference between the brains of homosexual and heterosexual men. His results were based upon his studies of 41 cadavers, consisting of homosexual men, heterosexual men, and women, along with the size of the hypothalamus, the area of the brain that governs sexual activity. His results showed the size of this area of the brain was similar in homosexual men and in women. As a result of this, LeVay concluded that the homosexual drive was biological.[15]

Numerous problems and objections exist with this study. First and foremost was the possible bias LeVay would have had as he studied, due to his homosexual lifestyle and the death of his homosexual lover to AIDS. Also damaging his results was the determination that, in some of the homosexual men, the size of the hypothalamus was the same as some of the heterosexual men. If homosexual behavior is linked to the size of the hypothalamus, then LeVay needed to explain why some men with the same size hypothalamus were heterosexual. He failed to account for this variability.

A third problem with this study is the dilemma of knowing what came first: did the size of the hypothalamus cause the homosexual behavior, or did the homosexual behavior cause a change in the brain? Studies have shown that the brain can be altered over time and through experience. An example of this is shown in those who become blind and begin to learn Braille: research has shown an increase in the size of the brain area used to control the reading finger. This should have been considered in the report offered by LeVay and his associates; however, it was casually left out as well. Simon LeVay would be forced to admit,

> *"It's important to stress what I didn't find.* ***I did not prove that homosexuality is genetic, or find a genetic cause for being gay.*** *I didn't show that gay men are born that way, the most common*

> *mistake people make in interpreting my work. Nor did I locate a gay center in the brain."*[16] *(emphasis added)*

Another significant study conducted was in December 1991 by Michael Bailey and Richard Pillard as they studied homosexuality in twins. They surveyed 56 pairs of identical twins, 54 pairs of fraternal twins, 142 non-twin brothers of twins, and 57 pairs of adoptive brothers. This study showed that 52 percent of identical twins of homosexual men were also homosexuals. Twenty-two percent of those who had fraternal male twins said their twin was also homosexual. Of those who were adoptive brothers of homosexuals, 11 percent claimed also to be homosexual. Their conclusion was that homosexuality is genetically determined.[17]

However, there are some major problems with the conclusions this study reaches. We obviously must ask why some of the identical twins, with the same genetic makeup, were not homosexuals. In 48 percent of the cases, those homosexuals with identical twins had a twin that was not homosexual. If genetics is to blame, then why were they not all homosexuals? Most published reports failed to announce that only nine percent of the non-twin brothers of homosexuals were also homosexual. Fraternal twins share as much genetic material with each other as they do with their non-twin brothers, so the discrepancy between the 22 percent for fraternal twins and the nine percent for non-twin brothers doesn't jive. When comparing the nine percent of non-twin brothers with the 11 percent of adoptive brothers, one can't help but see the inconsistency with the claim that homosexuality is genetics based. How is it that adoptive brothers, who share absolutely no genetic similarities, are more likely to both be homosexuals than non-twin brothers? Genetics can't be the reason.[18]

A team of researchers led by Dean Hamer of the National Cancer Institute released study results in 1993 announcing the connection of homosexuality amongst men to a gene, q28, on the X chromosome. Hamer's team collected information from 76 homosexual men, and

AGENDAS ATTACKING AMERICA PART 2

determined that a high level of the participants had homosexual male relatives on their mother's side of the family. A follow-up study of 40 pairs of homosexual brothers showed that in 33 of the pairs there was a distinct variation that occurred on a portion of the X chromosome known as q28. Their conclusion then was that homosexuality was linked to this gene and passed through the maternal line.[19]

While this study was trumpeted as the discovery of a "gay-gene", some major concerns have been raised with the reliability of the conclusions. One of the most significant concerns raised is that Hamer neglected to study whether any of the heterosexual men in the same families also had the variation on Xq28. If it did occur, this fact would definitely call into question the conclusions. Also, what about the other seven pairs of homosexual brothers that did not show the same variation or "gay-gene"? If the "gay-gene" had been discovered why was there not a 100 percent similarity amongst all homosexuals in the study?

While many took this particular study and ran to the media with the results, shouting at the tops of their voices that a "gay-gene" had been discovered, one of Hamer's co-researchers contacted The Office of Research Integrity in 1995 claiming the results of this study were not trustworthy and falsely represented due to research improprieties. The claim alleged that Hamer, in his efforts to locate males with Xq28, had decided to dismiss all the other males in his study who didn't have the gene, thus creating inflated research numbers that would support his desired conclusion of homosexuality being genetic. In 1998, in the January 30th edition of the *Washington Blade*, a Washington D.C. based newspaper that serves to advance the cause of the homosexual agenda, Hamer conceded that homosexuality is,

> "Culturally transmitted, not inherited... **there is not a single master gene that makes people gay.** ... I don't think we will ever be able to predict who will be gay,"[20] *(emphasis added)*

GAME PLAN

THROUGH THE LENS OF THE BIBLE

The issue of homosexuality is addressed very plainly in Romans 1:26 when Paul is addressing the Gentile refusal to honor God – exchanging the natural relation of man and woman for unnatural ones. What was Paul's measure for what is natural and what is not? If we simply remember that when God said in Genesis 2:18,

> "It is not good for the man to be alone; I will make him a helper suitable for him"

He created the helper in the form of woman (Genesis 2:21-25), then we can understand what is considered natural by the One on whom all nature depends. The Creator and Designer of all created the standard to be one man and one woman, coming together to live as husband and wife. It is this relationship that Paul uses as the "natural" and he describes any sexual relationship other than this as "dishonorable passions" and "shameless acts" worthy of death (Romans 1: 26-32).

Along with Paul's teachings in Romans, we also see a very plain and clear teaching on this subject in 1 Corinthians 6: 9-10. While inspired by the Holy Spirit, Paul makes it painfully clear that individuals who are practicing homosexuals will not be in heaven.

> "Or do you not know that the unrighteous will not inherit the kingdom of God? Do not be deceived; neither fornicators, nor idolaters, nor adulterers, nor effeminate, nor homosexuals, nor thieves, nor the covetous, nor drunkards, nor revilers, nor swindlers, will inherit the kingdom of God."

It's not that God doesn't love them, nor is it that the penalty of their sin can't be paid in full by the blood of Jesus Christ, through their turning to God in obedience to His will. The real problem lies in an individual who chooses to stay in a lifestyle that contains any of the above listed sins. That's the significance - they choose to stay there. We know that the Bible addresses homosexuality as a choice; in 1 Corinthians 6:11, it is referred to as part of a new Christian's past lifestyle. Once the person is "washed, sanctified, and justified", he is no longer as he once was.

> *"Such were some of you; but you were washed, but you were sanctified, but you were justified in the name of the Lord Jesus Christ and in the Spirit of our God."*

THE REAL ISSUE:

When the smoke clears and the catchy slogans wear off, the truth is that an agenda is being pushed in a major way. What was once thought of as sacred, the family as God designed it, is now looked at as old-fashioned and needing to change with the times. If you or the teens in your life speak up for what you know to be accurate, then you are considered intolerant and even painted as unloving.

It's not even about the science really. In April of 2003, The Human Genome Project was completed which was the nail in the coffin for those who had hoped to find a genetic reason for homosexuality. The scientists, after unraveling the genetic makeup of humans and looking for reasons for specific behaviors, homosexuality being one, all came to the same conclusion – there is no gene that dictates that one must be a homosexual. However, those advancing this agenda have and continue to push for more research to be conducted, looking for validation for this sinful behavior.

GAME PLAN

CHALK TALK: WHAT'S THE GAME PLAN?

1) Be aware!

Many of us live in our own little world of daily activities, and we aren't truly informed as to what is really taking place in the agenda of homosexuality. First, we must know what the goal is of those pushing and advancing this agenda.

2) Decide right now that your TV will not serve as an avenue for this agenda to be pushed.

Many of the "entertainment" outlets we have today are filled with pro-homosexual messages. In a society that is all about tolerance, the mass media will often present a slanted view toward homosexuality and away from a Christian worldview. If you choose to not throw the TV completely out, when homosexual references and news stories come across your set, make sure you take those "teachable moments" to discuss with your teen the way these groups are pushing the agenda and how should not be easily swayed by the "crafty doctrines" and opinions of men.

3) If your child's school has joined hands with GLESN, either get your child out of that school or become very involved in counteracting the indoctrination.

It's not about a political issue. Make sure you don't make it one. At stake are the hearts, minds, and souls of every child – including yours – in that school. Parents can volunteer, serve as sponsors of Christian clubs, and even sit down and speak with the principal about their

AGENDAS ATTACKING AMERICA PART 2

involvement. To simply throw your hands up in the air is not a game plan; it's a surrender plan. Get involved!

4) Include Those Wrapped Up in This Agenda in Your Family Prayers

The attitude you display on this issue before your children will be adopted by them. Make sure your children know that God's Word teaches us that He doesn't accept the sin of homosexuality, and that those who practice this lifestyle will not enter into heaven; however, go out of your way to also teach them that God sent Jesus to die for them as well. When you pray as a family, include those who are wrapped up in this agenda in your prayers. God will hear you and so will your children. Through this, you will teach them the value of the souls of those pushing this agenda.

GAME PLAN

CONCLUSION:

Let's go back to the book of Leviticus now. In chapter 19, God tells the children of Israel how to respond to the environment they would encounter in Canaan. The Bible reads,

> **1** Then the LORD spoke to Moses, saying: **2** "Speak to all the congregation of the sons of Israel and say to them, 'You shall be holy, for I the LORD your God am holy."

Holiness is a topic that far too many people misunderstand. It's not about slapping on a tie and sitting in a pew. In Leviticus chapters 18 through 20, you won't find a worship service or an instruction of a worship service to Jehovah God. In this section of Scripture, the main thrust is about holiness lived out. It's about what holiness looks like in everyday life. It's about what God expects from His chosen people – to live lives that are set apart and different, because Jehovah God is our Lord.

By Def·i·ni·tion

Holy —adj
1) consecration
2) effect of consecration
   a) sanctification of heart and life

What did it mean, then, to "be holy"? Simply put, it meant that the children of God were not to get involved with the immorality and the idolatry that was taking place in the land of Canaan. They were not to adapt and adopt the cultural lifestyle. They were to be a people that were following after God in everything, even if it meant that they would be isolated and not accepted by those around them.

The message is the same for us today. In a world where agendas are being heavily pushed, we must remember that we are to be a light that reflects glory back to God (Matthew 5:13). When someone looks at our lives, they are supposed to see something that is different. They will notice we live for a different purpose, to please God.

AGENDAS ATTACKING AMERICA PART 2

Remember, this world is not our home. We truly are just passing through. If we are going to live with God for eternity, then we must live with Him here and now on this earth, following the teachings of the New Testament out of a sincere heart and with pure motives.

> *"Be holy, for I the Lord your God am holy."* (Leviticus 19:2)

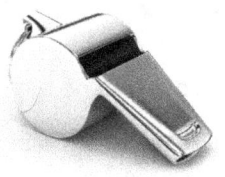

CHAPTER 7

WE MUST GET BACK TO...

If you've ever driven your car off the road, even just for a second while looking down at the radio or while turning around to reach for something in the backseat, you understand very well how terrifying it can be. Your senses are alerted as you grip the steering wheel just a little tighter and pledge to never do that again. You knew looking away from the road wasn't a smart idea, but at the time it seemed that what distracted you was very important. You quickly realize that while you're driving the car, there's only one thing that is really important: staying on the road and driving in a manner that is safe and according to the laws.

When we consider our current culture, it's no secret that we have driven off the road and into the median in some areas. We heard the rumble strips as a warning, or maybe we didn't because there were so many protestors and loud signs. It's possible that even though we knew what we were doing as a society wasn't the best, we had a spirit of apathy and assumed the changes really wouldn't hurt us that much. Now as we lift our eyes and refocus on where we are and where we're going, we realize maybe it really was a "big deal", and that we have relaxed too much in recent years. It's when we are shocked and alerted that we want to steer the car back onto the road, a steady and more secure pathway, so that those in

GAME PLAN

our vehicle will not suffer the consequences of a brutal and fatal crash.

Every society, past and present, stands on pillars that are its fundamental strength and support. These serve not only to add security to the rest of the policies and the behaviors within those societies; they serve as "zero", or the absolute beginning building blocks. If these pillars ever cracked or crumbled, the society felt it. If someone tried to move them, the society adjusted or fell apart. Their significance, looking through the lens of history, can never be understated. If they crumble, a brutal and fatal crash will follow. We must look up and observe. It's time we examine a few of the pillars that are key to America, and to each and every one of our children.

PILLAR ONE: STRONG FAMILY UNITS

"No amount of law enforcement can solve a problem that goes back to the family."

– J. Edgar Hoover

In Genesis chapter 2, as God watches his child Adam, He sees something is lacking in Adam's world. He has created for Adam a perfect garden to live in; He's given him food; and he's provided companionship through the animals... but there is still something missing in Adam's life. Since God is all loving and concerned with His creation, He states,

> **18** *"It is not good for the man to be alone; I will make him a helper suitable for him." (Genesis 2:18)*

It is significant to notice that prior to this point in the creation account, God has declared everything as "good". If God is the very standard of "good"– see Luke 18:19– then it stands to reason that anything He declared "good" was complete and at the highest standard. The very first time we read of something not being "good" in God's eyes was when man was found to be alone in the garden.

WE MUST GET BACK TO ...

There is actually a current case study of this in the world. About three decades ago China passed a law that is simply referred in English as "the one-child policy". As a method for dealing with the over-population problem in the country, this law limited most families to having only one child. Chinese officials are quick to point out that there are some exceptions to this law; however, the end result is a significant decrease in the number of children being born. The rate of baby girls in particular has dropped significantly, with China having no form of Social Security and families relying heavily on their young men to support elderly family members. This prolonged stifling of the natural balance has concerned many leaders in the fields of medicine, sociology, and criminology, and led to questions about the long term effects this policy will have on the Chinese society.

One such documentation of this concern can be seen in the September 15, 2005 issue of *The New England Journal of Medicine*:

"The Chinese government has acknowledged the potentially disastrous social consequences of this sex imbalance. The shortage of women may have increased mental health problems and socially disruptive behavior among men and has left some men unable to marry and have a family. The scarcity of females has resulted in kidnapping and trafficking of women for marriage and increased numbers of commercial sex workers, with a potential resultant rise in human immunodeficiency virus infection and other sexually transmitted diseases. There are fears that these consequences could be a real threat to China's stability in the future." [1]

Along with the problems listed in the above quotation, some Western scholars in this area of study have observed low-status young adult men with little chance of marrying and forming their own families, and have concluded that these young men are "much more prone to attempt to improve their situation through violent and criminal behavior in a strategy of coalitional aggression." [2]

GAME PLAN

Looking at the amount of data collected since the passing of the "one-child policy" in the late 1970s, one conclusion continues to ring loud and clear – It's Not Good for Man to Be Alone!

So, what's the answer to this problem? God's answer in Genesis 2 was good enough to solve the problem for Adam, and it's good enough to solve the problem today.

> **21** *So the LORD God caused a deep sleep to fall upon the man, and he slept; then He took one of his ribs and closed up the flesh at that place.* **22** *The LORD God fashioned into a woman the rib which He had taken from the man, and brought her to the man. (Genesis 2:21-22)*

When we think about the creative nature of God, we can't help but see both His goodness and thoughtfulness. For example, He created the environments on days one (light/darkness), two (heaven/sky was separated from the earth), and three (water/land separated, vegetation and fruit). Then, on days four (sun/moon/stars), five (creatures of the water/birds of the air), and day six (land dwelling creatures/humans), He created what would fill the environments. There were no accidents and there is absolutely no reason to believe God created what He did randomly or haphazardly. In the same way, there is good reason to believe that when God created woman from the rib bone of Adam, it was intentional.

Days of Creation

Environment	Inhabitants
Day 1 Light/Darkness	**Day 4** Sun/Moon/Stars
Day 2 Heaven/Sky	**Day 5** Creatures of the water Birds of the air
Day 3 Water/Land Vegitation/Fruit	**Day 6** Land dwelling creatures Humans

WE MUST GET BACK TO ...

By nature, the rib is a protective bone. It's not like the femur, or the long bone of the leg, which is designed to bear the weight of the body as well as add support for walking and standing. The rib bones instead, as they are wrapped around the vital organs of the body, serve to protect and to provide structure. If a rib bone breaks and turns inward, all of a sudden it becomes a sharp dagger with the possibility of puncturing a life-sustaining organ. If another bone in the body breaks, perhaps the radius of the arm, one of the lower arm bones, it will hurt, but the likely hood of your life being in jeopardy is not high.

Since God could have chosen any bone in Adam's body, we might be curious as to why He chose that one. Why not choose a little toe bone or even a bone of the head?

Taking into account the function of the rib bone, the Biblical description of woman as a "helper", and God's insight that it was not good for man to be alone, you have an idea of the answer. Woman was to be Adam's companion. Some would say she would, just like the rib bone, provide a protection of sorts to Adam, staying by his side and protecting him from the loneliness that would have been surrounding him as the only human. No matter how one defines it, woman was very significant to the problem of it not being good for man to be alone, as well as in helping fulfill the command found in Genesis 1:28,

> 28 *"Be fruitful and multiply, and fill the earth..."*

Family units have always been very significant. The Old Testament writer, Nehemiah, understood this significance when as a leader, he was faced with leading God's people in the rebuilding of the wall of Jerusalem around 445 B.C. Despite having enemies of the land threatening an ambush, Nehemiah calls all the workers together and places them in the holes of the walls in family units. Husbands and wives, sons and daughters- all worked side-by-side, plugging the hole to which their family had been assigned.

GAME PLAN

Nehemiah noticed their great fear and called the people together and said,

> **14** *"Do not be afraid of them; remember the Lord who is great and awesome, and fight for your brothers, your sons, your daughters, your wives and your houses." (Nehemiah 4:14)*

Nehemiah clearly understood the power of persuasion. He knew the people would gain strength if they could stay focused on the fact that God remained great and awesome, even through the exile, death, and destruction they as a nation had just endured. He also knew that placing the families together in the unfinished spaces of the walls would lead that family to fight harder and with a determination to protect the lives of their loved ones. Simply put, he declared it was "Time to Fight for Your Families!"

We need to take up Nehemiah's declaration today – it is time to fight for our families! According to Jennifer Baker from the Forest Institute of Professional Psychology, the divorce rate in America is between 45 percent and 50 percent for first marriages. While this percentage appears to be decreasing, we need to stop patting ourselves on the back. The reason for the divorce rate dropping may not be what we think.

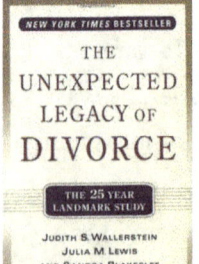

The impact of the divorce epidemic in our country has been well studied and documented by researchers such as Judith S. Wallerstein, who is considered by many to be the leading authority in the world on the effects of divorce on children. In her book *The Unexpected Legacy of Divorce*, Mrs. Wallerstein described the observations of a first-hand study she conducted. This study began in 1971 and included following and talking to a group of 131 children whose parents were all going through a divorce. Over the next 25 years, she was allowed access into the children's lives as they grew from adolescence into adulthood, observing

WE MUST GET BACK TO ...

their struggles and listening to their own statements about the real effects of the divorce in their lives. While not everyone in the study ended up the same, there are some commonalities that deserve attention.

> "National studies' show that children from divorced and remarried families are more aggressive toward their parents and teachers. They experience more depression, have more learning difficulties, and suffer more problems with peers than children from intact families. Children from divorced and remarried families are two to three times more likely to be referred for psychological help at school than their peers from intact families. More of them end up in mental health clinics and hospital settings. There is earlier sexual activity, more children born out of wedlock, less marriage, and more divorce. Numerous studies' show that adult children of divorce have more psychological problems than those raised in intact marriages." [3]

While, as Americans, we don't like hearing that we might be the cause of some of our own problems in society, the truth is – as the family goes, so goes the country. Since the 1960s, we have seen a steady increase in the number of violent crimes amongst teens, in the number of teen pregnancies, in the amount of teenagers who are reported as clinically depressed, in the number of school age children who are on some type of psycho-social drug to control behavior, as well as the number of children who are considered in need of special education classes. What has led to these trends in our country? Is it that in the "good-ol' days" people just didn't report the problems, or do we really have something to worry about? I would propose to you that the person who will stand and declare that these problems have always been there, and that the only reason we hear of them today is because of the media, has a valid point but they are missing the real issue. The point is not that we've always seen some of these symptoms present amongst the youth of our country. The real issue is that over the last 50 years, we have seen an increase in each and every one of these symptoms. To deny that is to bury our heads in the sand and pretend the real world is not happening around us. We can not help young people today if we refuse to admit where we are as a culture!

When we truthfully look at subjects like violent crime and gang activity, study after study demonstrates that virtually every major personal and sociopathic condition can be traced to fatherlessness. Dr. Stephen Baskerville, the past president of the *American Coalition for Fathers and Children*, reported,

> "When considering violent crime, substance abuse, unwed pregnancy, suicide, and others that fatherlessness far surpasses both poverty and race as a predator of social deviance."[4]

Our society continually tries to sell us a bill-of-goods by telling us that only poor people that have issues with violent crimes and drug abuse, and that they are at the highest risk for unwed pregnancies. The reality is all these are symptoms of a greater problem – fatherlessness. It's not a racial or a socio-economic problem. It's a father problem.

I've had many opportunities to work with teens in various settings and from various backgrounds. One such experience came when my parents served as house parents at a group home for troubled and neglected teenagers. In the three years I was there, living with eight to ten teenage boys at a time and working with them in the summers, I learned a different angle to one of hottest topics in American society – teenage violence through gang activities. Most, though not all, of the young men I was around and worked with in those three years had some type of checkered past with violence. Some had been gang members and some had simply been abused, sexually, physically, or mentally (often times there was a combination of all three); their way of handling it was lashing out in anger. Part of my family's responsibility while at the group home was to show these young men what a Christian family was and how we operated. Along with this, we also had to help them understand a better way to deal

WE MUST GET BACK TO ...

with their anger. The more I got involved and listened, the more I realized that their anger was a mask to cover a bigger issue. These young men, most of them at least, came out of broken homes and suffered from one of, if not the largest, epidemic facing our children today – abandonment.

CONSIDER THE FOLLOWING SCENARIO.

A woman gets pregnant and the dad is not in the picture, or perhaps the couple was never married and the father decides to leave. The mother then is forced to raise a child on her own. In America today, she can raise him one of two ways: either on welfare or by going out and getting a job to teach him to become a productive citizen of this nation. She decides to go out and get a job and in so doing, guess who's not there to make sure he gets off to school in time, or even has breakfast in the morning, or even has his homework done? The mother.

That young person is now faced with walking home from the school bus stop and continually facing two or three other guys who act out and intimidate him. In this situation, most young people would go home and be secure in the knowledge that their mom and dad are there to take care of them. They might even tell their parents about it, and the three of them would come up with a better plan of getting home from school. However, in this young man's life he doesn't have that security at home because no one is there for him. Mom is out working one or more jobs, trying to support her family. So what's the answer for this young man? He decides to go out and find two or three other guys that come from the same background so they can walk down the street together. Next time they encounter those two to three other guys, they are not as scared and intimidated. That's called a gang.

> **By Def·i·ni·tion**
>
> **Gang** —n
> a group of youngsters or adolescents who associate closely, often exclusively, for social reasons, especially such a group engaging in delinquent behavior.

GAME PLAN

While I don't make any excuses for gang behavior, during my family's time at the group home, I learned to better understand why some teen violence occurs. Those whom I have spoken with who have run in gangs enjoyed the money and power; however, when all the surface reasons for joining were laid out, the real nugget they were searching in joining was for security and family. They wanted to know someone "had their back" and that there would be a group of people to die along with them if it really came down to it.

The need for family is just as strong today, and possibly even more so, than it's ever been in America. Generation after generation has gone by, and gradually we have gotten to the point where we are today. Sadly, there are fewer and fewer teenagers who can even tell you of someone in their life who has been married for 50 years or more. The "happily-ever-after" concept is quickly becoming a thing of the past, and only a slight memory for some in America.

THE SHIFTING TIDE IN MARRIAGE

As was mentioned earlier, the divorce rate has decreased slightly over the years. We would love to celebrate this seemingly positive element in our current culture; however, the reason stifles any celebration that we might want to muster.

According to the National Marriage Project, since 1970 the marriage rate for those women 15 and older has decreased by over 50 percent.[5] Along with this, we are seeing a delaying of first time marriages until later in life. In 1960, the average age for first time marriages for males was 23 and for females, 20. Today, the average age for males is 28 and for females it is 26.[6] With this delay in getting married and with fewer people joining in holy matrimony, one has to wonder what alternative people in America have found in regard to our relationships. Are we simply dating for years on end? Perhaps we've just given up on relationships altogether and the

WE MUST GET BACK TO ...

human race in America is dwindling because we aren't having children. Or maybe, we've just decided that marriage is not as necessary as it once was, and as a society we are shifting towards the "new way of doing things" - cohabitation and having children out of wedlock.

Unfortunately, that's exactly what the trends are saying. In 1960, America saw roughly 450,000 unmarried couples living in our society. Since that time, the number of cohabiting couples, including same-sex unions, has increased over twelve times; we now have over 6.7 million unmarried couples living together, and over 40 percent of these households contain children.[7] The research also shows that well over half of all first marriages are now preceded by the couple living together, many of them having bought into the lie that you should "try it out" before entering into a contract like marriage. The current cultural lie is that by doing so, one can have a better chance of a successful marriage; however, that couldn't be further from the truth. To the contrary, most evidence shows that if a couple lives together before getting married and then they marry, their marriage is more likely to end in a divorce then a couple who did it the "old-fashioned" way.[8]

This shift in the acceptance of non-traditional families in America has not occurred without affecting teenagers. According to the most recent *Monitoring the Future* surveys conducted by the University of Michigan's Survey Research Center, 67.4 percent of high school seniors surveyed said they agreed with this statement: "It is usually a good idea for a couple to live together before getting married in order to find out whether they really get along."[9] In this same report, only 35 percent of high school seniors believe that marrying will result in a full and happier life as compared to staying single or simply living with someone.[10] Another telling effect can be seen in that over 50 percent of both teen guys and girls believe that having a child out of wedlock is a "worthwhile" lifestyle. To demonstrate how much has changed, consider that in 1970 only 33 percent of girls and 41 percent of boys thought this was a good idea.[11] Oh, how things have changed.

GAME PLAN

CHALK TALK: WHAT'S THE GAME PLAN?

1) Show your teenager what a Christian marriage is.

It's been said often that what you do speaks louder than what you say. This saying couldn't be more true than when it comes to family. Teenagers notice hypocritical teaching. They learn even when you think they have finished learning. Show them what a Christian marriage is. Give them the stability they desperately need during their teen years. You will also impact their dating and courtship in that their approach will be one of finding a future spouse that has the same commitment to making marriage last and making marriage God-honoring.

2) Introduce your teenager to Christian couples who have been married for 50 years or more.

It will greatly benefit your teenager to sit down with those Christian couples who have been through life's difficulties together and have remained committed to one another. Let your teen- sometimes require your teen- sit down and interview these couples. Let them find out what it takes to have a lasting marriage and what it takes to overcome struggles. Then, take your teen out to dinner, fathers and sons / mothers and daughters, and discuss with them what they learned. Parents are the most important people in the lives of even teenagers. Actively engage them and discuss with them what the Bible says about dating, courtship, and marriage.

3) Take a Family Weekend

Let's face it, sometimes we don't spend enough time as a family enjoying our family. We all go our separate directions in the morning, and we return to each other in the evenings; however, we don't get to spend much time just enjoying each other. You must take the initiative and plan a family getaway. It might be a long weekend fishing or possibly a camping trip. Maybe you are the type of family that loves amusement parks or venturing to a professional baseball game. Whatever it may be, we all must make a serious effort to spend time together - i.e. put it in the calendar of your phone and set the alarm to remind you.

PILLAR TWO: A NATION OF INTEGRITY

> *"Live in such a way that you would not be ashamed to sell your parrot to the town gossip."*
>
> *– Will Rogers*

A certain husband and wife wanted to help those who were in need. At the time, many church members were chipping in to help others, because there were so many away from their native countries who had risked everything when they decided to obey the Gospel message preached by the apostles. Those Christians who had any manner of material goods sold items so they could share with those who did not have anything. This husband and wife team decided they would sell a plot of land and give the money to the apostles. While this sounds innocent and very benevolent, and it was, the events surrounding the entire process would eventually cost both Ananias and Sapphira their lives - not because there was a great battle over the price of the land, nor because they were attacked by robbers, trying to get the money. Rather, both died because they lacked integrity, demonstrated when they lied to God (Acts 5:4).

GAME PLAN

Defined as "*conduct that conforms to an accepted standard of right and wrong*", integrity is one of those words, that while we have a written definition, is easier to define by examining situations and through watching the lives of people, especially when they don't know they're being watched.[12] For example, recently I was standing in line to pay at a pizza buffet. It was a Friday, and the restaurant offered a deal on Friday allowing kids six years of age and under to eat for 99 cents. As I waited, I observed a grandmother paying for two of her grandchildren. When the cashier behind the counter asked the children's ages, the grandmother replied that one child was 3 years old and the other was 6. Immediately the older child, wanting to make sure she was not short-changed, spoke up and said, "Grandma, I'm 7 years old." The incident caught my attention of course as I waited to see what the grandmother would do. To my surprise, both the mother and the grandmother immediately called the children to move down the line and began getting their food. Grandmother then told the child, as she tried to escape the "caught with the hand in the cookie jar" moment, "You mean, you'll be 7 soon…"

Those of us who have had small children understand that when an age is reached, a child counts it as an insult if someone doesn't tell their right age. To them it's important to make sure everyone knows exactly how grown-up they really are. Based upon this fact, the logical conclusion is that this grandmother and mother team wanted to save $2.00 so they lied about this young girl's age.

While both the Biblical illustration and the pizza buffet illustration might sound trivial to some Americans today, the truth is they represent just two of the small holes that have been carved through the once standard and strong pillar of integrity.

In times past, the pillar of integrity has served as a stable, strength for our communities as neighbors and in business deals. As time has progressed, and as court cases have demonstrated, a person's character is no longer acceptable without a legal document that backs it.

WE MUST GET BACK TO ...

Our society loves to call itself a "Christian" nation, which means we follow the teachings of God found within the Bible, and that we look to Jesus Christ as the redemptive Lamb of God. However, claiming something and being something are entirely different. One can claim all day they are a 6' 10" starting NBA basketball player, but unless you actually are, then it doesn't matter what you claim – reality is reality.

Christians, who the Bible refers to as children of God, ought to strive to be like our Father in the way we live and in the character we possess. In two very familiar verses describing an aspect of God's nature, the Bible says,

> **19** *God is not a man, that He should lie, - (Numbers 23:19)*
>
> ———
>
> **17** *In the same way God, desiring even more to show to the heirs of the promise the unchangeableness of His purpose, interposed with an oath,* **18** *so that by two unchangeable things in which it is impossible for God to lie, we who have taken refuge would have strong encouragement to take hold of the hope set before us. (Hebrews 6: 17,18)*

Most people would not expect Christians to lie, because, quite simply, they claim to serve a God who doesn't. The teachings found within the Bible also make it very clear that being a Christian and living a lifestyle that winks at lying don't go hand-in-hand; however, as a society that claims to be Christian, we have become very good at redefining what a lie actually is, even at times giving them colors to make them sound innocent (i.e. "white lie"), and coming up with reasons why sinning through lying is at times acceptable.

GAME PLAN

THE FACTS OF THE MATTER:

In a recent survey by the Josephson Institute Center for Youth Ethics, more than 40,000 teenagers were asked to answer a series of questions anonymously. The main objective was to discover what teenagers profess to believe and what they actually do to put their beliefs into practice. The results, while strictly teen related, represent a growing gulf in America. As a society, we love to boldly stand and claim to have a standard of morals, but when push comes to shove, often times those morals become limp like wet noodles.

Significant results of the study pointing to BELIEFS...

- **98%** - I believe it's important for me to be a person with good character.
- **98%** - In personal relationships, trust and honesty are essential.
- **93%** - In business and the workplace, trust and honesty are essential.
- **96%** - It's important to me that people trust me.
- **94%** - It's important to be thought of as ethical and honorable.
- **98%** - It's important to have good moral character.
- **84%** - It's not worth it to lie or cheat because it hurts your character.
- **80%** - My religion is important.
- **92%** – I am satisfied with my personal ethics and character[13]

WE MUST GET BACK TO ...

Significant results of the study pointing to ACTION...

- **80%** - *lied to parents about something significant*
- **83%** - *lied about something to save money*
- **61%** - *lied to a teacher one or more times*
- **81%** - *copied another person's homework*
- **59%** - *cheated on a test in the last year*
- **33%** - *use the Internet to plagiarize an assignment*
- **21%** - *stole something from a parent or relative*
- **18%** - *stole something from a friend*
- **28%** - *stole something from a store*[14]

Clearly a wide gap exists between what teens believe and what they do. Is it a matter of the maturity of the teenagers, or is it possible that teenagers are simply modeling what they see and hear around them? Has the culture of Bill Clinton's "I did not have sex with that woman" finally come to roost? Has the media's continual portrayal of deceit for the "right reasons" finally started to taint the moral color of our nation? The answer to all these questions and more is a resounding, "YES!" While we would be very naïve to try placing the lack of integrity amongst America's youth on one or two sets of shoulders, we can safely conclude that our society as a whole has not reinforced solid ground when it comes to this issue.

Consider a night of family entertainment around the television. CBS's *Survivor* comes on and the family mindlessly pays attention and roots for their favorite. Through all the challenges and the tribal counsels, the family misses the major theme - the one who can form the alliances and deceive the most people wins the $1,000,000 prize. Sure, some will claim this is only a game and that it really isn't lying if that's how one plays the game; however, is that not justifying a behavior? If we can comfortably justify lying in this case, does it become easier to justify lying in other cases as well?

GAME PLAN

Recently the National Endowment for Financial Education, along with Forbes.com, commissioned a poll conducted by Harris Interactive. The findings do shed some light on the great gap between what teens believe and what they do. Is it possible that teenagers are simply modeling what they see in the adults in their lives? One of the most significant results of the survey found that 31 percent of the adults admitted to having been deceptive to their spouse or partner about money. Of these...

- **58%** - *hid cash from their partner or spouse.*
- **54%** - *hid a minor purchase from their partner or spouse.*
- **30%** - *hid a statement or a bill from their partner or spouse.*[15]

While not every parent or teacher falls into the category of having lied to their spouse about money, this is simply one example of many that demonstrate that lying is not simply a teenage problem. Unfortunately, as we age and mature, the studies show that we don't really outgrow the problem of deceit. Teenagers notice every time an adult in their life "stretches the truth" or "exaggerates the truth". They catch the lifestyle that doesn't add up to the professed beliefs, and the lesson is reinforced that it's possible to believe one thing and act in a way that is contrary. This is a lesson demonstrated all too well in the Josephson Institute Center for Youth Ethics survey, with 84 percent of respondents said, "it's not worth it to lie or cheat because it hurts your character" yet 59 percent admitted to having cheated on a test in the last year.[16]

THE TRUTH OF THE WORD:

In John chapter 8, Jesus is confronted by the scribes and Pharisees who are challenging Him about His claims to be of God. In response to their claim that they only have one Father and that is God, Jesus explains to these religious individuals,

WE MUST GET BACK TO ...

> **44** *You are of your father the devil, and you want to do the desires of your father He was a murderer from the beginning and does not stand in the truth because there is no truth in him. Whenever he speaks a lie, he speaks from his own nature, for he is a liar and the father of lies. – (John 8:44)*

Jesus' message here is hard to miss. These scribes and Pharisees were claiming to be children of God, but they weren't listening to Jesus who spoke the Words of God. Since they subscribed to lies, Jesus explains to them that they look a whole lot more like the devil than they do God the Father.

To us, the message is very clear as well - lies do not originate from God but rather from the devil. If we, as individuals, claim to be Christians and thus children of God, then why is it at times we look a whole lot more like the devil than we do our heavenly Father? Why is it that America can claim to be a "Christian" nation, yet based upon the words of Jesus, and through observing survey after survey, when we look in the mirror we see anything but God the Father? Through our attempts to redefine what it truly means to be a "Christian" and even a "Christian" nation, we have failed to change the words of Jesus. Lying still originates from the devil, and until that sin ceases to reign in our marriages, in our families, and in our culture, society will continue to crumble as the once strong pillar decays and remains broken.

GAME PLAN

CHALK TALK: WHAT'S THE GAME PLAN?

1) Eliminate the Negative Influences.

Nobody ever said meeting the enemy on the field of battle was going to be easy. If that were the case, he wouldn't be much of a challenge nor a threat to our children's eternal destination in heaven. Realizing that your children and those you work with are constantly watching and learning, even when you think they aren't paying attention, you must take ownership of the possibility that you have been a negative influence in demonstrating integrity to them. If you're going to help your children in this area, you must first repent and change your thinking, resulting in a change of your actions. What seems innocent can have eternal consequences. Don't be that millstone (Matthew 18:6)!

Stop watching shows that glorify sin. I realize that sounds pretty pointed and might be offensive; however, think about the messages that are being sent under the guise of simple entertainment. As it's been said, children are sponges and they are soaking it up! The question is, what are they soaking up from the media- and is it helping them get to heaven?

2) Show them the positive.

There is great value in children seeing adults practice integrity even when it's not popular. The next time the cashier gives you too much money back, bring it to their attention and give the excess back. If your waiter doesn't charge you for an item, bring it to his/her attention and let them know you want to pay for what you ordered. These seem small, but they will have a big impact on your child. I will always encourage you to point out the Bible passages pertaining to God's view of lying; however, in our society, it's not that we don't know we shouldn't lie. We just don't care. You have got to show the children in your life that you do care. Show them what integrity looks like.

WE MUST GET BACK TO ...

3) The "Small" Must Become "Big"

Most of us overlook the small things. While this might work when we're cutting the yard or cooking dinner, it is not healthy when it comes to teaching our children the importance of always telling the truth. There are no small lies. As a matter of fact, if we do not correct our children when they tell small lies we teach them that it's okay. We must make the "small" lie a "big" deal. We must teach our children that God doesn't see a lie in the same way we do.

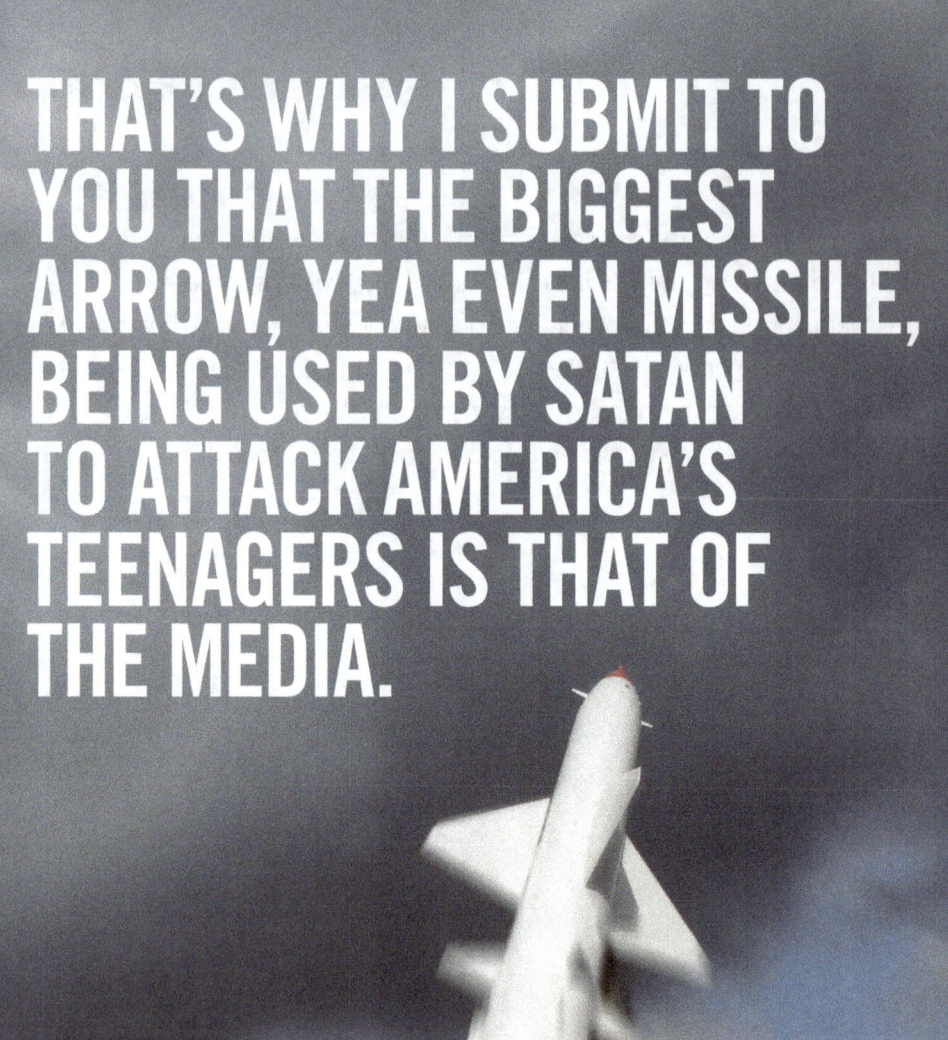

CHAPTER 8

THE ATTACK WE'RE UNDER ...

What is the largest missile Satan is using to attack the American teenager today?

In Ephesians chapter 6, the Bible tells of a very serious and deadly war that is waged against the Christian, one with eternal consequences.

> **10** *Finally, be strong in the Lord and in the strength of His might.* **11** *Put on the full armor of God, so that you will be able to stand firm against the schemes of the devil.* **12** *For our struggle is not against flesh and blood, but against the rulers, against the powers, against the world forces of this darkness, against the spiritual forces of wickedness in the heavenly places.* **13** *Therefore, take up the full armor of God, so that you will be able to resist in the evil day, and having done everything, to stand firm. – (Ephesians 6: 10-13)*

The apostle Paul's charge is very clear – Get Ready to Stand! He knows that the war is taking place, even if the Ephesians aren't ready. That's why he tells them in verse 14 to put on the full armor of God. If they think they can take on the "schemes of the devil" and stand against the "spiritual forces of wickedness" alone, they are bound for failure, and will die spiritually. Unfortunately, with the wrong perspective, this sad realization won't hit them until they take their last breath here on this earth.

In order to be prepared for this battle, Paul instructs them to put on Truth and Righteousness. He tells them to make sure their feet are covered with the Gospel of Peace. The helmet of Salvation is a must, and the Sword of the Spirit is what they will use to defend and to attack. In the midst of this very specific description of the spiritual armor of God, Paul defines the shield as Faith in verse 16. It's with this aspect of the armor of God that the Christian will be able to absorb and extinguish the flaming arrows that Satan is hurling at them.

My question to you is, what does this look like in modern day America? In Hebrews chapter 4 verse 12, the Bible claims to be living and active. It's not just some ancient book that sits on a shelf, but one that is relevant in our society today and in your life. So what does it look like when the Bible says to take up your shield of Faith because the devil is going to be throwing some flaming arrows at you? He's going to be launching missiles at you and the teenagers in your life, and you've got to ask, "Where are those coming from and what do they look like today?" Are we to assume that the evil one is stuck in a time period of sandals and cloaks? Does he even know what's going on today in our society and what we as Americans are so wrapped up in? Is it possible that this war is still being waged today against those who claim to follow Christ?

I submit for your consideration today that Satan still hates God, and that he would love nothing more than to steal from the hands of God as many souls as he possibly can. I also propose that the methods he uses today aren't that much different then what he used in the Garden of Eden when he tempted Eve with the fruit that was a "delight to the eyes" (Genesis 3:6). Therefore, when we consider Satan's arrows, we might assume most Christians would be able to recognize them and be prepared to raise their shields against them. However, the sad fact is, just like Eve reasoned to take the bite of forbidden fruit, we reason and justify our lack

THE ATTACK WE'RE UNDER ...

of a response to the largest arrow that Satan has, even as he continues to launch it at our families and specifically at our teenagers.

THE BIG MISSILE CALLED MEDIA

According to a recent Kaiser Family Foundation national survey, Americans ages 8 to 18 years of age devoted 6 hours and 21 minutes every day with media in 2005. With media multi-tasking, using multiple media devices at the same time, they managed to actually shove 8 hours and 33 minutes worth of media consumption into that time. According to this same survey, teenagers today allow media entertainment to consume on average 7 hours and 38 minutes of their day, with actual media consumption being the equivalent of 10 hours and 45 minutes each day. *(These rates do not include time spent on computers in school, talking on the phone, or time spent text messaging.)* The only other activity that might get more attention in their daily lives is that of sleep.[1]

Part of the reason for this increase of over 2 hours more of actual media consumption each day is technological advances such as smartphones, which act as an all-around media consumption device. When we compound the availability of media outlets with a culture that seems to push towards operating more and more in the technological realm, it's not a major surprise to see this shift. The days of blackboards and books are not becoming a thing of the past- they are already ancient in the minds of today's teens. They still are being taught and are required to read, but what we are noticing is that advances in technology are taking over even the classrooms, which spills into ever facet of their lives. Books are quickly being replaced by e-readers, and pen and paper are quickly being replaced by tablet computers.

To understand just how much media is a part of the everyday life for today's American teenagers, consider the following:

GAME PLAN

- **66%** of 8 to 18 year olds have a cell phone
    - 33 minutes/day spent talking on cell phone
    - 49 minutes/day listening to music, playing games, watching TV
    - 90 minutes/day texting
- **31%** of 8 to 10 year olds have a cell phone[2]
- **76%** of 8 to 18 year olds have an iPod or other MP3 players
    - On average, teens 15 – 18 spend 3 hours and 3 minutes every day listening to music.[3]
- **29%** of 8 to 18 year olds have their own laptop
    - 17% of 8-10 year olds have their own laptop
    - Average use of computers for teens, outside of school related usage, is 1 hour and 29 minutes a day.
    - Social networking sites such as Facebook and MySpace consume the majority of teenagers' time on a computer.
- **84%** of homes with teens present have Internet access
    - 33% of these teens report having Internet access in their room
    - 36% of 8 to18 year olds have a computer in their bedroom[4]
- **99%** of homes with teens present have at least one TV
    - 79% of these homes have 3 or more TV sets
    - 71% of teens report having a TV in their bedroom
    - 84% of these homes have cable or satellite
    - 47% of these homes subscribe to premium channels such as HBO and Showtime
    - 24% of teens in these homes have access to these premium channels in their bedrooms

THE ATTACK WE'RE UNDER ...

- Young people with a TV in their bedroom spent an average of about 1-hour more per day watching live TV than those who do not.
- 37% of teens report having a video screen in the family car[5]
- **87%** of homes with 8 to 18 year olds present own a video game console
  - On average, these homes have 2.3 consoles each
  - 8 to 18 year olds spend on average 1 hour and 13 per day playing video games
  - 49% of the time playing is on a console
  - 23% of the time playing is on a cell phone
  - 29% of the time is on a handheld player
  - 50% report having a video game console in their bedroom[6]

The American culture today truly is one big information highway that streams in constant information about relationships, gender identity, values, sex, families, and peers just to name a few. This huge open door to America's youth surely doesn't go unnoticed by the one, Satan, who would love nothing more than to steal your children's innocence and purity. That's why I submit to you that the biggest arrow, yea even missile, being used by Satan to attack America's teenagers is that of the media.

Before you tune me out, I want you to know that I am not anti-media. I believe that media has some good purposes.

- *Media introduces us to different cultures.* I don't have to go to China to know something about it. I can get the Internet anytime I would like, and research the Ming Dynasty or see pictures of the Great Wall.

GAME PLAN

- *Media unifies us around major events.* Both in cheerful and sorrowful events, we gather around media for entertainment and to learn more. Think of Super Bowls, World Series, and even the attack on the World Trade Towers on September 11, 2001. In all these, there are groups of people who are united by the media and the events they cover.

- *Media is a great tool in education.* Teachers produce presentations they use in their classes, as do some preachers for the delivery of their sermons. Audio CDs are sometimes used to teach a foreign language. Documentaries are shown to reemphasize the importance of a particular event in history.

While there's no doubt that media can be used in a very positive way, we must not live with blinders on, refusing to see what else can come along with this tool. Both sides of the coin deserve attention, and there's plenty of negative that comes with the media as well. When you consider the shift that has taken place in American values and in morality, it shouldn't surprise anyone who's ever watched or listened to the most popular shows and musical artists today.

- *Media desensitizes us.* If I hit my thumb with a hammer one time, it hurts. However, if I hit my thumb in the same spot over and over again, eventually it won't hurt as bad because the feeling has been lost. The media has a way of showing us images of violence, sex, and other impurities in numerous ways. With minds that absorb what is put in front of us, it's no wonder that scenes, or lyrics, or presentations that would have embarrassed audiences 50 years ago are now commonplace and offers very little shock value.

- *Media presents an unreal view of life.* This is part of the reason we like the media, as it separates us from our everyday lives. However, life is really not all about drinking, shooting, and engaging in sexual encounters with numerous individuals. It isn't always about

solving serious problems in a 30-45 minute time frame where emotionally we are left with a message that all problems should be able to be solved quickly, and if they can't then there must be something seriously wrong. Off the silver screen, sometimes it takes days, weeks, months, and possibly years to address some of the problems we encounter in life.

COMPONENT ONE: THE TELEVISION

I want you to think for a moment about the set up of your living room at home. You see the couch, the chairs, and possibly a coffee table or two. The family pictures hang on the walls or set on the bookshelves in the corner. Maybe there's a fireplace on one wall with a decorated mantel. Are you mentally there? Great! Now what's the one item that all of those pieces of furniture are positioned around? Meaning, what truly drove the purpose of the layout of your family living room?

If yours is like most homes in America, the answer is most definitely the television that hangs on your wall or sits in the entertainment center. What once was not even a part of the American culture, has become the centerpiece of the room we settle down into every night before we go to bed. We host gatherings in this room, and at times, those parties even center around what comes on the TV. Our evening schedules, depending on the particular night, are often planned around what shows come on. Family nights have taken on the image of a glowing box showing the movie of the night as the family sits together on the couch.

The fact that so many households in our culture own televisions is not the main issue, unless buying the biggest high-definition flat screen television leads us to sacrifice giving to the Lord, or if watching the television consumes all the time that could be given in service of the Lord and His church. The major threat comes into play when we consider what comes over that captivating screen.

GAME PLAN

In July 2010, the U.S. Second Circuit Court of Appeals handed down a ruling in the case of *Fox Television Stations v. FCC.* Many of the major broadcast networks joined with Fox in this effort to counteract the authority of the Federal Communication Commission (FCC) to regulate what can and can not be shown in television shows. In other words, these major broadcast stations didn't want anyone telling them what decency laws must be enforced, especially those laws that pertained to the use of profanity. In their ruling, the Court struck down the FCC's attempt to handle the "fleeting expletives" by enforcing fines, thus opening even further the floodgates of immoral filth that could come across the TV – even during what is commonly known as the "family-hour" (8-9 PM).

The Parents Television Council, in their efforts to inform and fight against the filth and garbage coming into our homes via the TV, recently released a report entitled *Habitat for Profanity: Broadcast TV's Sharp Increase in Foul Language.* In this study, the PTC compared the level of profanity in the fall of 2005 with the fall of 2010. What they discovered was exactly what Andrew Schwartzman said would happen. Schwartzman, the head of *Media Access Project,* a legal organization serving on behalf of the entertainment industry in the above case, said after the results of the hearing,

> "There's no question that this decision is going to mean more [explicit content]... They're already much more aggressive about trying to get stuff in."

What were the results of the PTC's study?

- Across all networks, use of profanity on primetime broadcast entertainment programming increased 69.3 percent from 2005 to 2010.
- The greatest increase in the use of the harshest profanities occurred in the "Family Hour" (8-9 PM).
- Across all networks and all hours of primetime, use of anatomical and sexual reference increased an average of 137 percent.
- Fox Television led the charge for changes, with use of profanity just during the "Family Hour" increasing by 268.91 percent.[8]

THE ATTACK WE'RE UNDER ...

Alongside the huge increase in vulgar and profane language, we have seen a significant increase in the quantity and the graphic nature of sexual content as well. In 1998, 56 percent of the shows on TV contained some type of sexual content, with 3.2 scenes per hour containing sexuality. In 2005, that number had increased to 70 percent of the shows containing some type of sexual content, with 5 sex scenes per hour.[9] With shows such as MTV's *Jersey Shore* and *Hard Times of RJ Berger* leading the charge, the number of sexual references among shows that are specifically geared towards young people, have increased to levels that your grandmother would have never dreamed about.

When considering the component of the television, the subject of media violence also merits attention. The American Academy of Child and Adolescent Psychiatry's website recently contained an article that reported, on average, there are 812 acts of violence shown on television every hour. Amongst shows that have children as their primary audience, mainly cartoons, the study reports 20 acts of violence per hour. They also report that by the age of 18, the typical American child, with average viewing time, will witness over 200,000 acts of violence in their selected television programming, including well over 10,000 murders.[10]

COMPONENT TWO: THE MUSIC

In the days of old, superstars such as Perry Como, Elvis Presley, and The Platters ruled the stage. Teenagers would flock to the various venues to hear the latest and hottest groups. Adults were concerned then, as we are today, that the lyrics and the beat of the music would incite teenagers to get up and move- or worse, to move to the back seat of a car. However, even the most progressive artists of that era recognized the importance of some boundaries, and they didn't dare go beyond them. That is not the case today. Modesty boundaries in dance moves, lyrics, and clothing (or lack thereof!) have been shattered, and there are no apologies being made.

GAME PLAN

According to recent reports from The Nielsen Company, the most preferred genre of music in America today is Pop Contemporary Hit Radio (40%). The second most popular genre is Rhythmic Contemporary Hit Radio (33 percent).[11] When we look at both of these combined, we can quickly see that our teenagers are downloading whatever is playing on the radio in the Pop/Dance genre. So the question is...What exactly are they listening to? With the reality being that adolescents use music as part of their identity formation, doesn't it make you curious to know what exactly what is piped into their heads when they put in those ear buds?

According to the current *Billboards Top 100* list, one particular song spent seven weeks at the top of the charts during the first quarter of 2011. It became the fastest-selling single in iTunes history, selling 1 million downloads in the first five days of release.[12] The song is entitled "Born This Way" and is sung by cultural icon – and yes she has become such – Lady Gaga. The song begins with these lyrics:

> *It doesn't matter if you love him, or capital H-I-M*
> *Just put your paws up*
> *'cause you were Born This Way, Baby*[13]

Through the exciting beat, the listener is over and over again inundated with the message that you were born a certain way, so be happy in who you are. It's a message that sounds good, especially in a culture where we are continually told that teen suicides are on the rise and that bullying amongst teens is increasing, both signs of a society of low self-esteem. However, when the Christian parent looks more closely at just exactly what the lyrics are teaching, the immorality oozes from the speakers.

> *No matter gay, straight, or bi,*
> *lesbian, transgendered life,*
> *I'm on the right track baby,*
> *I was born to survive.*[14]

THE ATTACK WE'RE UNDER ...

Another song that has made a splash in the Pop Contemporary Hit Radio genre is entitled "S&M". The artist, Rhianna, is no stranger to the news. The night before the 2009 Grammy Awards, she and then boyfriend, Chris Brown, got into an argument that turned violent. Brown ended up hitting her and leaving her on the side of the road. Rhianna told *Rolling Stones* in a recent interview that, from that moment on,

> "I put my guard up so hard. I didn't want people to see me cry. I didn't want people to feel bad for me. It was a very vulnerable time in my life, and I refused to let that be the image. I wanted them to see me as, 'I'm fine, I'm tough.' I put that up until it felt real."[15]

With her desire to show a stronger side, and to change public perception of her, Rhianna unleashed *Rated R*, an album that contained songs about murder and revenge. She then would go on to further confront the public perception of her as a weak and helpless woman by releasing *Loud*, which blurs the lines between sex and violence. This album also contained "S&M", a song about masochism, in which the chorus of the song states,

> *Cause I may be bad, but I'm perfectly good at it*
> *Sex in the air, I don't care, I love the smell of it*
> *Sticks and stones may break my bones*
> *But chains and whips excite me.*[16]

Along with the sexually charged lyrics of many songs in this genre, music videos intensify the messages of the songs, especially concept videos – videos that tell the story of the song instead of showing content from a live concert. In times past, many adults were concerned with the content that was broadcasting across channels such as MTV, BET, and CMT. Their concern came with good reason, with 75 percent of those concept videos involving sexual imagery, and more than half involving violence, usually against women.[17] Fortunately, as time has passed, not only has the location where teenagers are getting their videos changed to outlets such as YouTube, but the videos have also moved, as a whole, away from imagery of violence directed at women. However, as far as the sexual content and storylines have gone, they have only slid further down the scale of immorality. Videos showing mid-drifts, cleavage, and tons of high cut outfits showing lots of leg have become commonplace, especially where the lead singer is a woman. Add to that female nudity from the side view, provocative dance moves, and men and women rolling around together on the bed or on the beach and a parent's nightmare has become a reality – imagery meets lyrics in a way to drive home the often times sexually charged message of the song.

If you're the parent of a teen or you work with teens, you're probably hearing the statement, "But I don't listen to the words; I like the beat." Rest assured that your teens aren't the only ones who have ever said those words or used that argument to justify listening to particular songs. However, this claim doesn't moralize listening to immoral lyrics. Aside from the fact that by downloading the song, or even by listening to the radio station that plays it, they are contributing financially to the production of more material like that, studies show that teens catch the meaning and the message behind the music and thus Satan accomplishes what he wills with this component.

> *Numerous studies have shown that aggressive words can prime aggressive thoughts, perceptions, and behavior. Indeed, such effects can occur even when the stimulus has not been consciously recognized. Further more, listeners are capable of recognizing themes of music (i.e. violence, sex, suicide, and Satanism) even when it is difficult to comprehend specific lyric content.* [18]

THE ATTACK WE'RE UNDER ...

COMPONENT THREE: THE INTERNET

Of all the possible pieces that together comprise the missile called Media, the Internet is probably the one that parents need to pay attention to most, and the one that has the most potential for destruction. With television and music, most parents can tune in or listen in and hear first hand the ungodly messages that are being thrown at their children. They are more blatant and obvious, easier to detect and thus easier to deal with when they come across your teen's eyes or ears. However, the Internet is accessible in ways that many times parents aren't even aware. With such a possibility of secrecy, Satan often finds it easier to slip in and have his way.

Compared to 2004, teenagers report using their computers an average of 27 more minutes every day. They spend roughly 1 hour and 29 minutes on the Internet daily with the number one usage being social networking – namely Facebook.[19] When you also consider the fact that more and more teenagers now own a portable device capable of going online, such as a cell phone, iPod touch, or some type of game system, the Internet is the fastest growing avenue for media consumption.

With social networking comprising the most Internet usage by teens, it is crucial that parents and other adults who work with teens be aware of just exactly what it is and why teens are attracted to it. Study after study will show that teens need to be connected to people. Most have a connection to their parents; however, as children progress through adolescence their need for peer-to-peer relationships increases. With this shift in attention, teens today are turning to various outlets that allow them to be connected literally almost 24 hours a day. While being connected seems to be a shift that will only grow as this generation of young people continues to age, it's what they're sharing and who they're sharing with that concerns us as adults.

A recent survey conducted by Common Sense Media found that there is a great divide in the dangerous activities some teens are participating

GAME PLAN

in through social networking sites and what parents think their children are participating in. While many teens find good ways to use social networking sites (join a group to support a cause, post creative writing, share positive videos, organize charity events, conduct Bible studies, invite their friends to worship, and volunteer for service projects), we are also seeing a trend in which teens use the social networking sites as forums for gossip, bullying and blowing off steam. Some are using it in ways that are even possibly more destructive.

- **37%** have made fun of other students (18% of parents think this is taking place)
- Nearly **one in five** teens (19%) say they have been harassed online or "cyberbullied"
- **16%** have posted false information or lies about other people (4% of parents think this is taking place)
- **28%** have shared personal information about themselves they would not normally share in public (16% of parents think this is taking place)
- **25%** have created a profile with a false identity (12% of parents think this is taking place)
- **24%** have hacked into someone else's social networking account
- **13%** have posted naked or semi-naked photos or videos of themselves or others online (2% of parents think this is taking place)
- **24%** have sent or posted pictures of someone else that they were not sure if the other person would have wanted shared
- **18%** have pretended to be an adult while chatting with someone online (8% of parents believe this is taking place)
- **39%** have posted something they later regretted (20% of parents think this is taking place)[20]

THE ATTACK WE'RE UNDER ...

Along with social networking sites, teenagers are flocking to online videos. The primary site for this is YouTube – ranked third in web brands only behind Google and Yahoo!.[21] This avenue of media consumption is so rampant that 81 percent of teens say that have watched videos online at sites such as YouTube, and of the total time teens spend with the computer each day, it consumes 16 percent of their time.[22] With the increase in cell phones that contain access to YouTube and with more teenagers owning their own laptops, this medium is one that parents had better take very seriously. Trying to keep it fair and balanced, I do want you to know that as with any media medium, sites such as YouTube can be used for good. However, as parents and adults who work with teenagers and who want these young people to be shaped spiritually in accordance with the Word of God, we must understand the dangers of online video sites as well.

For instance, in looking at the top YouTube videos for 2010 – with Justin Bieber's *Baby* taking the top spot with 406 million views (over 1 million per day) – we see that six out of ten contain immodest dress, provocative moments, profanity in the lyrics, or violence. If that isn't enough, those who watch these and other videos are able to leave comments below the videos that could at times make even a sailor blush.

In 2008, the Parents Television Council conducted a researched effort to expose the amount of inappropriate material showing up on YouTube. In their report entitled *The "New" Tube*, they found that after looking at just the top 20 "teen idols" there were 422 instances of explicit content within the text commentary. An average of 68 percent of those comments included profanity and 31 percent of the profanity was of the most offensive nature. Search terms such as "Hannah Montana" and "Miley Cyrus" produced the highest percentage of sexual references and violent references in the text commentary. Disney's "High School Musical" showed the highest percentage of profanity (77 percent).[23] The study clearly demonstrated that teens don't even have to search for immorality and profanity; it is showing up in places that most parents wouldn't be concerned with.

GAME PLAN

The most obvious danger with the Internet is the readily available, highly charged sexual material of pornography. On numerous occasions, after completing one of my weekend seminars, I have had a teenager come up to me asking for help with their addiction to this deadly poison. Many of them are guys, but I have had girls talk with me who either were struggling or had struggled in their life with a pornographic addiction. It's very sad to me to see how Satan can pervert and twist something that God made both to be beautiful and appealing to our nature as humans. Teenagers' hormones, newly kicking in, and their sexual development, are easy prey to the potential sin that waits for them in this online world.

According to Google Trends, in 2007 a search for the word "sex" would have brought up just under a half of million pages (425,000). Today, conducting the same search for the same word results in 1.7 billion pages, an increase of over 4,000 percent just in a little over 3 years. With the other hundreds of words that could be used in searches for immoral websites, there's no question why so many children report having visited pornographic websites.

According to the web based group, Family Safe Media,

- Average age of first time exposure to Internet pornography is 11 years old.

- Largest consumers of Internet pornography are young people between 12 and 17 years old.

- Young people ages 8 to 16 who have viewed pornography online is as high as 90% (most while doing homework).

- Young people 15 to 17 years old who have had multiple exposures to hard-core pornography is as high as 80 percent.[24]

Most young people who are exposed to Internet pornography didn't go looking for it the first time. With more and more school assignments being given out online or turned in online, the likelihood for these encounters to happen has increased considerably. Pornography is no longer something one has to go into the corner convenience store and purchase, all the while embarrassed that they actually have to put the magazine on the counter and the clerk will see their face and know what they are buying. Today, if a child is searching for something as innocent as a toy or even doing an historical report on our government, some of those search terms are linked to pornography. Once the child sees it, hopefully they will immediately click out of it and go and tell their parents. However, we don't live in a sinless world, and sometimes curiosity gets the best of a young person. If they click the link just to see what it is, all of a sudden they are taken across the World Wide Web and entangled in a world they never intended to enter into the first place. If they stay there, their minds will be altered. Their perception of healthy sexual relationships will be damaged, and the likelihood of them having failures in their future marriages will increase significantly. All while Mom and Dad sit idly by without a clue that their perfect little child is wrapped up in this addiction.

THE DESTRUCTION LEFT BEHIND

With all of these "less-than-wholesome" images and lyrics coming into just about every home in America, we shouldn't be surprised that what young people allow into their eyes and ears impacts who they become. Jesus Christ pointed to this very fact in Matthew chapter 15 when He said,

> **17**"Do you not understand that everything that goes into the mouth passes into the stomach, and is eliminated? **18**"But the things that proceed out of the mouth come from the heart, and those defile the man. **19**"For out of the heart come evil thoughts, murders, adulteries, fornications, thefts, false witness, slanders.

The Biblical principle of sowing and reaping is clearly seen in this passage as Jesus was teaching His disciples about the Pharisees' issue with Him eating without washing His hands. When something is on the inside,

GAME PLAN

it will display itself on the outside through behaviors and attitudes. The Pharisees were so concerned about the outside and making it appear clean by customary practices, but they had missed the most important message of making the inside, the heart, clean in order to make the man clean. In other words, what you see in a person's life stems from what is inside their heart. Work on the inside, and the outside will take care of itself. This same principle is not simply a New Testament concept as Solomon speaks of it Proverbs 4:23, when he says,

> *23 Watch over your heart with all diligence, For from it flow the springs of life.*

Since the heart of an individual is so significant, and with Jesus teaching that outside behaviors are an indication of what's on the inside, doesn't it stand to reason that if we continue to allow the teenagers in our life to ingest ungodly content, they will eventually produce ungodly behaviors and attitudes? One would think that a Christian parent or a youth worker would get that point, and many do; however, I am increasingly amazed how many times adults will play the "my child can disassociate" card when they are gambling with their child's eternity.

A group of researchers from the University of Michigan picked up a study that began in 1977 by surveying 577 children from the Chicago area. The study measured the amount of TV violence the children ingested along with the level of aggression they expressed with confronted with a stressful situation. Over the next 15 years, most of these children were followed into their early 20s and some into their 30s, as researchers tried to discern whether or not exposure to media violence as children had affected them as adults. Taking into account and neutralizing as much as possible other factors, the research all pointed to a hard fact:

> *"One can see that men who were high TV – violence viewers as children were significantly more likely to have pushed, grabbed, or shoved their*

spouses, to have responded to an insult by shoving a person, to have been convicted of a crime, and to have committed a moving traffic violation... men who were high TV-violence viewers in childhood were convicted of crimes at over three times the rate of other men."[25]

The same report went on to report on women exposed to high levels of media violence as children:

"Women who were high TV-violence viewers as children were more likely to have thrown something at their spouses, to have esponded to someone who made them mad by shoving, punching, beating, or choking the person, to have committed some type of criminal act, and to have committed a moving traffic violation... women who were high TV-violence viewers as children reported having punched, beaten, or choked another adult at over four times the rate of other women."[26]

Another study conducted by the Rand Corporation solidified the Kaiser Family Foundation's statement that, "young teens ranked entertainment media as their top source for information regarding sexuality and sexual health."[27] Since teens are saying they are learning about sexuality from the media, one could expect to see, as the Rand Corporation pointed out:

- *Teens who watch a lot of television with sexual content are more likely to initiate intercourse in the following year.*
- *Television in which characters talk about sex affects teens just as much as television that actually shows sexual activity.*[28]

Isn't it interesting that as sexual content has increased both on the television and in the world of music, much less the astronomical boom seen on the Internet, that teens' sexual activities have increased as well? Just take a look around your teen. Look at what their peers are wearing, at how marketers are trying to influence them, and at some of the celebrities that are attracting them. Sexuality has become more mainstream and

GAME PLAN

out in the open as compared to 50 years ago. With this increase, Satan is taking advantage.

In Matthew chapter 22 and verses 34-37 the Bible reads,

> **34** But when the Pharisees heard that Jesus had silenced the Sadducees, they gathered themselves together. **35** One of them, a lawyer, asked Him a question, testing Him, **36** "Teacher, which is the great commandment in the Law?" **37** And He said to him, "YOU SHALL LOVE THE LORD YOUR GOD WITH ALL YOUR HEART, AND WITH ALL YOUR SOUL, AND WITH ALL YOUR MIND."

This particular passage is one of those that come at you like a train. You see it coming, but many times aren't as tuned into what it really says as is needed. We, like the lawyer in this Scripture, want the CliffsNotes version (or today, the SparkNotes version) of what God desires from us. Here, in answering this lawyer's testing question, Jesus simply tells him to love God with everything that is possible for humans to love him with. It's the same message that God told the children of Israel in the Old Testament when He said,

> "You shall have no other gods before Me (Exodus 20:3)

For the most part, parents and teens have a logical understanding of the message Jesus was delivering here. We know that if we want to inherit eternal life that we must love God with all our heart. We even have songs that are written about this very thing, trying to encourage our young people to put God as first priority in their lives. We understand very well that our soul will one day depart from our bodies and will go to one of two places. Therefore, we obey the simple teaching of the Bible and respond out of faithful obedience, being baptized so that our sins can and will be forgiven. However, while we find it very easy to claim we know what it

THE ATTACK WE'RE UNDER ...

means to love God with all our minds, we find it very difficult to actually put that knowledge into practice.

Part of the reason is because we live in a society filled with media that is teaching anti-God messages or lifestyles and quite frankly we just don't want to choose to leave those TV shows, music, or Internet material out of our lives. Of course we would never verbalize that. If we were even asked that on an anonymous questionnaire, we would never admit that; however, where we do admit it is often times in the fact that we watch the same TV shows, go to the same movies, listen to the same music, and look at the same Internet sites as does the rest of the world. Our uniqueness as Christians seems to only be unique in that we might put a coat and tie on and go sit in a pew on Sunday mornings; other than that, our practices are all too similar with those who don't claim to follow after Christ.

THE PHILIPPIANS 4 CHALLENGE

Think about Philippians chapter 4 and about the concept the apostle Paul is teaching about mindset when he writes,

> *8 Finally, brethren, whatever is true, whatever is honorable, whatever is right, whatever is pure, whatever is lovely, whatever is of good repute, if there is any excellence and if anything worthy of praise, dwell (set your mind) on these things.*

What is your first reaction? I immediately asked myself why Paul was telling Christians where to set their minds. Shouldn't they know where to set their minds? Why did he need to remind them?

The Scriptures do this over and over again for those who want to follow after Christ. In Romans chapter 12, Paul instructed the Christians,

GAME PLAN

> *2 And do not be conformed to this world, but be transformed by the renewing of your mind, so that you may prove what the will of God is, that which is good and acceptable and perfect.*

The reason for all this attention on what to do with the mind is very simple – our minds determine our actions; therefore if God has our minds, He will have our actions. Think about it: sin first occurs inside of us. Growing up, if your parents told you not to do something, but you really wanted to do it, you had to struggle with that internally so you would not have to struggle with it externally because of the effects of discipline. Being a Christian is the same way because our human nature is a part of us. We want to do what God does not allow – that's sin (lawlessness) and we are all guilty of it. Therefore, as we grow and mature in our faith, we change our thought process away from us and more towards HIM so that our lives line up with the Light.

That's what Paul wants from the church in Philippi. He wants their minds to be set on the right things, so their lives will be what God wants. That's exactly what we are called to do today. That's exactly what you as parents and youth workers have to make sure you are helping to foster when it comes to the teens in your life because Satan is not waiting around for us to get our acts together; he is coming after our teens now. The less involved you are in the area of media when it comes to your teens, the better it is for Satan.

Let's go back to Ephesians chapter 6. We are told to pick up our shield of faith so that we can extinguish the flaming arrows of Satan. For many young people their faith is still developing. Many are not mature enough, spiritually speaking to be able to ward off a lot of the attacks that Satan throws their way. It's not the natural tendency of a hormonally charged teenager to run like Joseph did from the topic of sex. Teens want to be included with their peers and often that means being able to discuss the

THE ATTACK WE'RE UNDER ...

music, the shows, and even the Internet sites. That's why it is crucial for you, as the adult, to hold your shield of faith over them while their shield is being prepared.

CHALK TALK: WHAT'S THE GAME PLAN?

1) Get involved in media habits of your child.

One of the biggest fears of most parents is that their child will not like them. Again, I don't think we would ever verbalize that, but we want to "leave the door" open for communication, which often times means being their friend. According to studies, parents are still the number one influence in the lives of teens. They respect you and will continue to respect you even more when you guide them in the way that God would have you to. Will they always like it? Do you even have to ask? Of course not. However, when they grow older will they be grateful you placed boundaries on them? Absolutely. So, don't be afraid to restrict time with media (that means all kinds). Also, you can't be afraid to turn off the media or change the channel when something inappropriate comes on. Talk with them about why you did it. They might not understand it now, but they will when they grow up.

2) Take the computer out of their room.

More teens get wrapped up in either overuse of media or else inappropriate use of media when the computer is in a private place like

GAME PLAN

a bedroom. You might have filters on there, and have set the parental controls to levels even you can't bypass, but rest assured, the talk at school and a few Internet searches can help any teen get around those small inconveniences. Love them enough not to put your teen in a position to possibly fail.

3) Change your own media habits.

If you really want your teens to take you seriously, you might have to change what you are modeling to them. If you tell them to turn off a movie that contains a sexual act, and then they see you watching something on TV that contains the same thing, they are simply going to think, "Hypocrite." Philippians 4:8 is not only directed at young people who want to follow God. It's directed at us too.

4) Use teachable moments.

You will never protect your teen from every negative thing out there. That's why I recommend using teachable moments. When a song promoting immorality comes on the radio, turn it off and ask your teen if he knows why you turned it off. Tell him you are trying to keep your own ears pure. Make it about you, recognizing that your example is powerful. Don't be afraid to bring the Bible into the conversation. Your teen needs to know that you value what God's Word says, and that you want him to as well. Use those teachable moments to train.

5) Discover a Positive Way to Use Media

As I told you in the opening of this chapter, media has some really good uses. Why not spend time as a family discovering positive ways to use it? Host a family game night where media is used, or come up with a way to use media to teach the Gospel. We can look at media

THE ATTACK WE'RE UNDER ...

as a tool that can be used for good or for bad. Why not teach your children how they can use it for good?

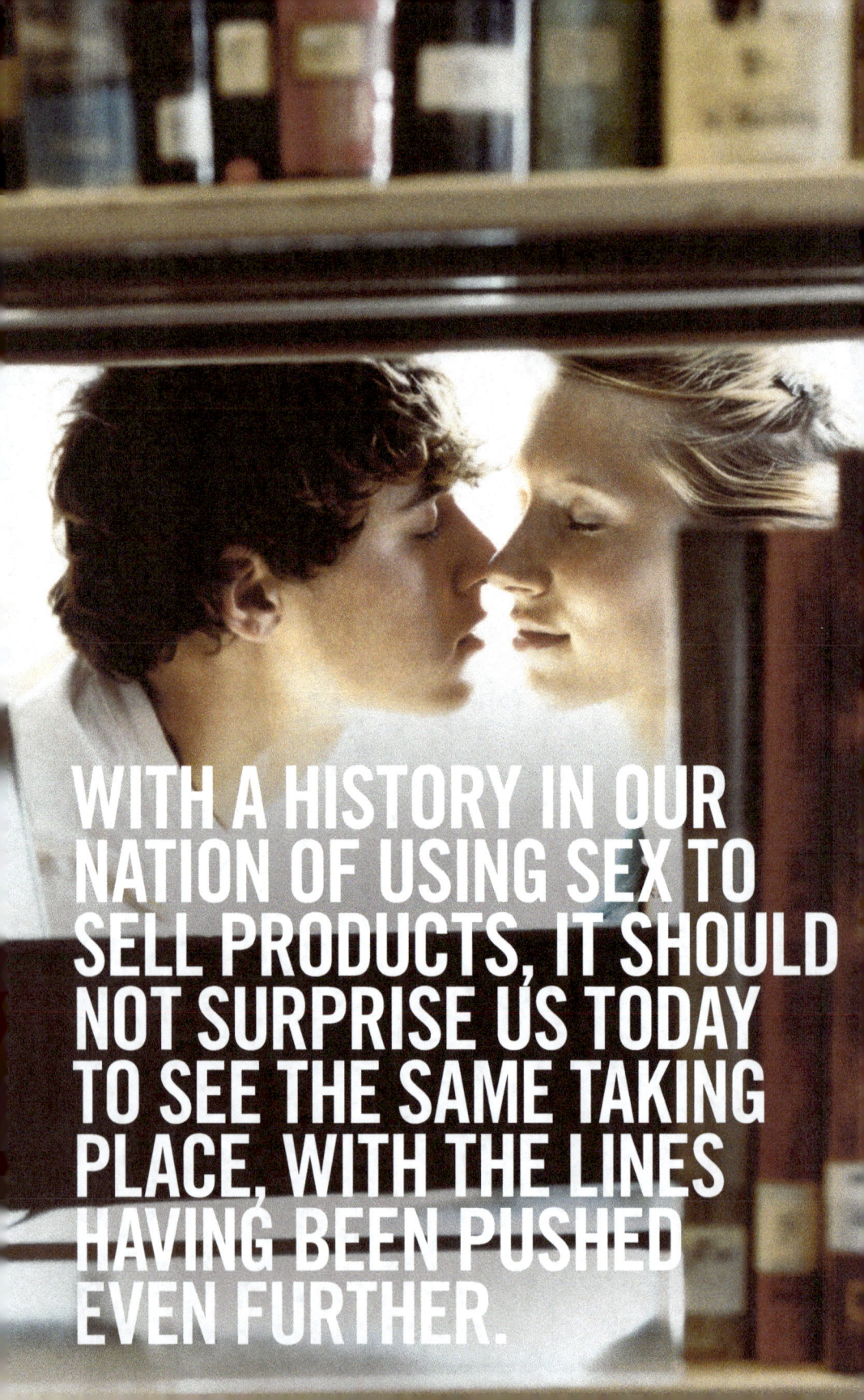

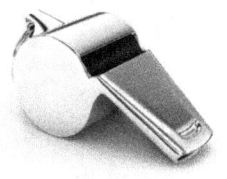

CHAPTER 9

THE SEXUALIZATION OF AMERICA

Her name is Ella Gunderson, and in 2004, this Redman, Washington, 11-year old decided that enough was enough. She reached her boiling point while on a shopping trip at Nordstrom's department store with her mother and sister, where she discovered that wearing the "in fashion" clothing stocked in the store would require her and other girls to show off parts of their bodies that should be reserved for their future husband's eyes only. As her sister, Robin, was trying on jeans the group found that "the style" was to either wear them entirely too tight or where they rode too low beneath the hips. Their concerns weren't relieved at all by the clerk who was helping them; she only encouraged Robin to buy the smaller size so she could have "the look" – meaning tighter and more revealing.

It was this conversation that inspired Ella to take action and draft a letter to Nordstrom's expressing her concern:

> "Dear Nordstrom, I am an eleven-year-old girl who has tried shopping at your store for clothes (in particular jeans), but all of them ride way under my hips, and the next size up is too big and falls down.
>
> "I see all of these girls who walk around with pants that show their belly button and underwear. Your clerks suggest that there is only one look. If that is true, then girls are supposed to walk around half naked. I think that you should change that."[1]

GAME PLAN

That letter made its way to Pete Nordstrom, who was at the time the president of Nordstrom's full-line stores. In response, the company ensured Ella they would try to educate the purchasing managers and salespeople on the wide variety of fashion choices that should be available to young people.

> **By Def·i·ni·tion**
>
> **sex·u·al·iz·a·tion** —n
> to render sexual; endow with sexual characteristics.

Ella's case demonstrates the growing attack on our teens, especially our young ladies. This attack is taking no prisoners, and is causing many girls to doubt their beauty and their worth. This attack can simply be described as the sexualization of our children. Its teachings drive home the point that outside of sexuality, a person is nothing. Its message is that we as humans are defined by what we look like, how appealing we are to the opposite sex, and what we are willing to do sexually. This attack causes eating disorders for many of our teens. Our young men have become addicted to working out, sculpting the perfect biceps, or worse yet, taking steroids, in order to meet society's supposed expectations. Grades are affected, alongside attitudes toward parents. Ultimately, purity is sacrificed when the brainwashing is complete.

If you don't believe this is happening in America, or if you think that this is an overreaction, consider the following cases and honestly reflect on whether or not we, as a culture, are teaching our youth to tie their identities to sex.

May 2002 – Outrage erupted over clothing store Abercrombie & Fitch's release of thong underwear made for little girls. If that weren't bad enough, these underwear are decorated with cherries and heart candies and some have the words "Wink, Wink" and "Kiss Me" across them.

As conservative groups across America pressured to have these removed, Abercrombie & Fitch spokesman Hampton Carney released a

THE SEXUALIZATION OF AMERICA

statement inciting even more concern: "It's not appropriate for a 7 year old, but it is appropriate for a 10 year old." The company would also say, "Once you get about 10, you start to care about your underwear, and you start to care about your clothes."[2]

December 2008 – New Rochelle High School, New York, became headline news, as reports of censorship and destruction of the novel *Girl Interrupted* were splashed across the Internet and heard over the talking head shows.

What was the story? A school official in the high school decided that the senior English students didn't need to read pages 64-70 of the book, which contained explicit references to oral sex. "The material was of a sexual nature that we deemed inappropriate for teachers to present to their students," said English Department Chairperson Leslie Altschul. "Since the book has other redeeming features, we took the liberty of bowdlerizing."[3] So…the pages were ripped from the book and the study continued, without the explicit scenes.

What was the response? Two days later, after a massive amount of scrutiny, the School Board announced that ripping the pages out in a measure of censorship was the wrong action to take, and that the books were to be reordered and studied in their entirety by students who chose not to opt out of the assignment.

March 2011 – Abercrombie & Fitch decides to launch a padded push-up bikini top on their website "Abercrombie Kids", a site that focuses on young girls ages 7-14. Once this was blasted on the news wire, Abercrombie & Fitch decided to change the marketing terminology, but they're still selling the same product, obviously seeing nothing wrong with suggesting that little girls wear something to accentuate this portion of their bodies.[4]

May 2011 – What ever happened to a mother's intuition? Brittany Campbell, an 8-year old girl from San Francisco, receives Botox injections in her face every three months to get ride of her "wrinkles". Brittany's mother is on a quest to make her daughter a beauty queen, and she feels

it's necessary to make her daughter's face "perfect". One might question whether the way God made Brittany's face might be considered perfect, as opposed to the way society says her face should look. So much brain washing has now taken place that little Brittany has stated, "My friends think it's cool I have all the treatments and they want to be like me. I check every night for wrinkles, when I see some I want more injections. They used to hurt, but now I don't cry that much."[5]

MARKETING SEX TO OUR KIDS:

Think about the last time you walked through a store such as Target or Wal-Mart. As you walked through the personal hygiene section and perused the deodorants and heavily scented soaps, how did you differentiate them? What stood out about the brand on the shelf?

If you're like most in America, you want to make purchases that will work for you and your body. You might like a particular scent, or possibly even the way you feel after you use the product. While we would love to think that most people simply respond with logic and common sense when it comes to these purchases, not everyone does- in fact, advertisers are banking that more and more Americans don't.

The cold hard truth is that when it comes to perfumes, colognes, clothes, and a number of other items, the minds behind the influence – the marketing and advertising departments – know just exactly what buttons to push, and they play off our over-sexualized society. They know the teenage boy wants to be attractive to the girls at his school, so their body spray commercials show women as animals seeking to devour the "prey" (which happens to be the young man wearing that company's body spray). Women are set up to believe that if they wear a certain perfume their confidence will be boosted and that men won't be able to resist them – demonstrated by the confident women being held close to a man in many print ads. Clothing lines make a habit of showing half-naked men or women to impress their message in the mind of the consumer, "I will look

THE SEXUALIZATION OF AMERICA

like that too if I wear those clothes" or worse yet, "Girls will want to sit on my lap with their shirts unbuttoned and lean back to kiss me if I wear those jeans too."

Sound crazy yet? If it is an overstatement, then why do so many companies use sex to sell their products? Why do they play off our insecurities and our desires if they will not add anything to their company's bottom line?

It's time to wake up and get our heads out of the sand. Choosing to ignore reality never helps us handle reality. The truth is, sex is selling and our children, teens, and even our spouses are being influenced by it every day.

The idea of using sex to sell products is not a new concept. As much as we may like to believe that Tommy Hilfiger and Calvin Klein have always had the market on sex and advertising, that's simply not the case. Even as far back as 1871, companies such as Pearl Tobacco used naked images of women on their containers to attract the male consumer. In 1898, R & G Corsets, in an attempt to capture the female audience, used an image of a woman in one of their corsets in a print ad, a highly sexual image for the time. The Rockford Varnishing Company circulated an ad in trade publications between the 1930s and 50s that showed a completely naked woman sitting on top of a piece of furniture under the title "Eye Appeal".[6] They described the lines of the human body in a way that is meant to allure the attention of the male audience. If they get their attention, then maybe the men will want to buy their product. At least they will think of their product when standing before a shelf full of options.

With a history in our nation of using sex to sell products, it should not surprise us today to see the same taking place, with the lines having been pushed even further. What turned the heads of consumers in the 1800s and the early 1900s unfortunately would not attract much attention at all today. Thanks to the desensitization of consumers, advertisers have had to increase the amount of flesh as well as add a sexual element to the appearance of the models or the images. Facial expressions, body postures, and concept of clothes falling off an individual give our highly sexualized culture a desire to learn more or to see more. The eyes in the ad express a desire for the consumer that is meant to draw a person in. It truly goes beyond a shock factor of nudity, and hits at a major indoctrination that we are seeing from every angle – a sense of not only being interested in sex in a natural way, but of being sexual in every way and in every thing we do.

SEXUAL EDUCATION AND THE MEDIA:

Would it shock you to walk into your child's elementary classroom at school and find a nurse teaching your little girl about sex? What about a health teacher showing your son how to use a condom? That's exactly what's taking place every year when you opt for your child to have sex education from a humanistic viewpoint. Granted, every school in America might not address the issue of sex education in the same way, and some might even stress the need for abstinence; however, in our culture, the not-so- shocking truth is that we are teaching 3rd and 4th graders about sex.

Why do we feel the need to teach them at such young ages? Is it because nearly every media outlet in America is issuing the argument, "Well, they're going to have sex before too long so we might as well inform them how to protect themselves against pregnancy and diseases"? Is it because when we see the behavior of people (both real and fictional) on TV and in magazines, we start to believe there are some things we just can't help, and sexual activity among teens being one? When will parents stop throwing their hands up in the air in defeat? When will solid Christian homes begin to realize that there are teachers coming into their homes every day, tutoring their young girls to become sexual objects and twisting their sons' ideas of how they're supposed to look at girls?

In a 2003 report entitled *Young People, Media and Personal Relationships*, by London University's Institute of Education, 66 percent of young people

THE SEXUALIZATION OF AMERICA

ages 10 to 14 said they learned about sex from the media. At that time, this statistic was headline news because for the first time, there was an admittance that young teens learned just as much about sex from the media as they did from their own mothers.

The shocking truth is that over the last decade, this statistic hasn't changed much as the amount of sex in the media has increased and become much more graphic and blatant. Whether it be talk of a little pill that can help a man with an erection problem, or a commercial that shows a woman either taking her clothes off or putting clothes on over her underwear, sex is out there and is no respecter of the age.

In a recent report on the subject of sexuality and media, the American Academy of Pediatrics echoed this conclusion:

- **75%** of prime-time programs contain sexual content, yet only 14 percent of the incidences mention any risks or responsibilities to the sexual behavior.
- Talk about sex on TV can occur as often as **8-10 times per hour**.
- **40%** of lyrics in popular music today contained sexual material.[7]

While the obvious places to look for sex in the media are TV, music, and the Internet, they aren't the only avenues for this indoctrination. Another such media outlet is video games. Today's teenagers are spending roughly an hour more per day on video games than they did just ten years ago. Much of this increase is based on what they can hold in their hand – a cell phone or hand held gaming device.

One of the top video games amongst teens, *Guitar Hero/Rock Band*, is a perfect example of how sexuality is slipped into some of the most unassuming places. In this particular game, your teen is invited to pick a rock star avatar (character) as well as the attire they will wear and guitar they will play. Through this process, children of all ages are exposed to

female characters with heavily accentuated breasts protruding from their outfits, bodily curves meant to attract, as well as larger than life eyes – all of which psychologists will report are sexual areas for humans. If you think your child hasn't played this game, it might shock you to find out that 71 percent of young people between the ages of 8 and 18 have admitted to picking up the plastic guitar or drum set.[8] I wonder what images were burned into their minds.

Roughly one out of every four video games depicts women as sex objects. In a report from the Media Awareness Network, it was revealed that

- **38%** of female characters in video games are "scantily clad"
- **23%** show bare breasts or cleavage
- **31%** have exposed thighs
- **31%** have exposed stomachs or midriffs
- **15%** expose their behinds[9]

With games such as *Super Mario* that are available to children, one would think that all parents could relax and not have to be worried about the sexual messages being relayed through this outlet. The problem is most teens today aren't playing *Pong* and *Frogger*. Games today, such as *Grand Theft Auto* and the *Sims* series, allow teenagers to see virtual nudity and participate in sexual activities through the avatars. The days of *Duck Hunt* and the original *Zelda* are no more. The limits have not simply been pushed back. They've been blown wide open with the dynamite of this agenda.

To find another avenue in which the media sells sexuality to our children, we can go directly to the checkout counter at the local grocery store. How about that magazine rack that many of us have tried to hide from our children, because of the covers that mainly show women in clothes that aren't leaving much to the imagination? Magazines such as *Vogue, Seventeen,* and *Cosmopolitan* have led the way in sexualizing America, as they flaunt airbrushed models and headlines of dieting and sexual fantasy before their female readers on a monthly basis. Are there no other topics that women are concerned with, or is this simply one more way of teaching women that outside of their bodies and what they do with their bodies sexually, they are worth nothing?

If archeologists in the future dug up a container that was filled with some of the most popular magazines on the shelf today, what would their conclusions be about women of our current society? Would they see a woman who was valued for her walk with God, or even for her thinking skills? Or would they think of a woman who was looked at as a sexual object? What conclusion would they draw from the fact that most magazines covers discuss two topics – weight loss and sex?

You and I both know the answer to those questions, and it ought to concern us when the American Academy of Pediatrics reports that in teen magazines alone, an average of 2.5 pages per issue are devoted to sexual topics. It should make the hair on the back of your neck stand up when you realize that coverage of sex as a health issue in magazines is more common than on TV, and that the predominant focus when it comes to sex in teen magazines seems to be on deciding when to lose one's virginity, not focusing on waiting until marriage.[10]

THE EFFECTS SEEN IN SOCIETY: HEALTH RISK

She's a freshman in college who looks in the mirror and only sees fat – although she is not overweight. This obsession with her looks causes her go days at a time without eating much at all. Then, the gorging begins. Chocolate cake, pizza, soda, and anything else she can afford is shoveled in. Moments later, before there is much time for anything to settle, she

makes her way to the restroom, where she leans over the toilet. Through her tears, depression, and fears, she gags herself and vomits the only food she's eaten for days. Sound like a scene from a horror film? It is! The only problem is that this script is not fictional.

To the unaware adult, the whole issue of America's sexualization might seem to simply be about modesty and the rate of teen sexual activity and teen pregnancy. While these subjects definitely deserve serious attention, especially from a Biblical perspective, they aren't the only areas that need to be addressed. The argument that every teen is having or will have sex before they leave high school is simply not true – although we are sadly not far from the tipping point as 46 percent of all high school seniors in America report having had sexual intercourse, and 14 percent have had four partners or more.[11] The revealing truth is that more than 46 percent have engaged in some type of sexual activity (oral sex, masturbation, etc.) with another person. The problem is, with those in high political offices redefining what sex is, most teens believe these activities don't count as sex; therefore, they believe that those who participate in them are still "technically virgins". The innocent kiss on the cheek at the end of a date has quickly been replaced by activities that rob our children of their purity and scar them forever – hurting their future relationship with their spouse.

According to the American Psychological Association, this issue of impressing sexuality as a means to define our young people is wreaking havoc, particularly in teens' cognitive and emotional development. Study after study has shown that self-objectification detracts from the ability to concentrate and focus one's attention – leading to decreased performance in logical reasoning and activities such as solving mathematical problems. It undermines confidence in and comfort with one's own body, which can lead to a host of possible consequences – shame, anxiety, and even self-disgust. Eating disorders and low self-esteem can follow, leading to depression and depressed moods.

The continual bombardment of sexual images in magazines and

THE SEXUALIZATION OF AMERICA

continuing talk of the "ideal sexual body" have driven many of our young people, guys and girls alike, to only see themselves for the fat that is on their bodies, regardless of whether they are at a healthy body composition. Dieting has become the latest craze, as we are continually told how overweight and out-of-shape our children are. While there's no denying our society has a problem with eating too much – one too many fries in the Happy Meal and not enough apple dippers - this obsession is causing serious mental health issues which are spilling out into relationships, into the schools, and even into our society as a whole. When 80 percent of 13 year old girls report having dieted, somewhere our society has lost balance. Health is a great thing to reach for – unfortunately, the more common goal is the body that Hollywood says you have to have, for the purpose of showing it off or using it as a sexual object.

SEXTING

A fifth grader slips off casually to the restroom, with her teacher's permission. Most people wouldn't think anything about this everyday school occurrence; however, times have changed and so have the games that teens are playing. This particular young lady is involved in a game in which she takes a picture with her cell phone of her nude body from the waist up, being very careful not to show her face. The picture is then sent to the juniors and seniors in the high school to be circulated around by the boys. The rules are pretty simple: whoever can guess whose bare breast are in the picture gets to have sex with the girl.

By Def·i·ni·tion

sext·ing —v
the act of sending suggestive text messages via a mobile device with the hopes of a future sexual encounter.

Is this for real? You had better believe it is, and it's not just one girl or one boy playing the game. The ready availability of cell phones to teens has opened an entirely different world when it comes

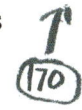

GAME PLAN

to sexuality. While some teens in days gone by might have thought about taking a Polaroid picture and passing it around, the amount of exposure and the possibilities of it being posted on the Internet were not present. It truly is a new game, and the over sexualized society we live in has birthed a generation of young people who for the most part, see nothing wrong with playing.

The topic simply known as sexting is one that has reached the national headline news over the past five years; however, there are still some adults that might be wondering just exactly what it is. Simply put, sexting is using one's cell phone to send sexually suggestive messages, partially nude pictures, or fully nude pictures. It's a modern form of flirting and at times serves as an open door to the casual sexual encounters that some teens today refer to as "hook ups".

Recently, The National Campaign to Prevent Teen and Unplanned Pregnancy and CosmoGirl.com conducted a survey with 653 teens (ages 13-19) to discover the amount of teens who are actually or have been involved in sexting at some time. Their results showed that

- **20%** of teens say they have sent or posted online, nude or semi-nude pictures or videos
- **22%** of teen girls
- **18%** of teen guys
- **39%** say they have sent or posted sexually suggestive messages
- **37%** of teen girls
- **40%** of teen guys
- **48%** claim to have received a sexually suggestive message

Who are they sending these pictures to? The same study revealed that...

- **71%** of teen girls and **67 percent** of teen boys have shared sexual messages or pictures with a boyfriend/girlfriend.
- **21%** of teen girls and **39 percent** of teen boys have shared sexual messages or pictures with someone that they were interested in or wanted to "hook up" with.
- **15%** of teens have admitted to sending or posting nude or semi-nude pictures via the Internet to someone they knew.

The study also investigated why the teens were sending these messages:

- **51%** of the girls who sent images did so because they felt pressure from a guy; **18%** of guys said they felt pressure from a girl.
- **66%** of girls and **60 percent** of guys said they did so because they wanted to be "fun and flirtatious".
- **52%** of girls sent them as a sexy present for their boyfriends.
- **44%** of teens sent a sexually suggestive message because they received one and felt they needed to respond.
- **40%** of teen girls sent images and messages as a "joke".
- **34%** said they did so because they wanted to feel sexy.[12]

As a father, my heart aches to think of so many teen girls and boys who have given into the sexualization in our culture. Where did they get the idea that, at the age of 14 and 15, they're supposed to be sexy? Why is it that in order to be "fun and flirtatious", nude images or sexual messages must be sent? Where did this teaching come from?

The answers to these and many other questions can be summarized by observing the life of an individual who from 2006 to 2011 captured the hearts of preteen guys and girls as one of the top television celebrities.

GAME PLAN

Within that timeframe, she and her TV show were nominated for over 40 awards, and won 23 of them. To whom am I referring? The one and only Miley Cyrus – or is it Hannah Montana?

In 2011, Miley Cyrus publically announced the end of the *Hannah Montana* train. A persona and a product line that had reached world-wide fame was now in the rearview mirror. Miley had her singing and acting career ahead of her, but there was one problem – she had to break out of the *Hannah Montana* mold. How would she do it? The answer became pretty obvious when at the 2009 Teen Choice Awards, in very high-cut shorts, she danced on top of an ice-cream cart against a pole, moving as if she were a stripper. The criticism came with force, and Miley, without backing down said in a *Parade* magazine interview,

> "My job first is to entertain and do what I love, and if you don't like it, then change the channel. I'm not forcing you to watch me. I'm not forcing you to talk about me. I would do that pole dance a thousand times again, because it was right for the song and that performance."[13]

Since that "coming of age" display, Miley Cyrus has continued to dress in highly sexual ways and release music videos with heavy sexual tones. Songs such as "Can't Be Tamed" and "Who Owns My Heart" are examples of the direction Miley Cyrus has chosen to break out of the mold.

Whatever happened to Hannah Montana, the squeaky clean image that Miley had, and at one time vowed to uphold? Where did she learn the lesson that if someone wants to change their image and attract an older audience, she has to start wearing body suits on stage and gyrating her hips when she dances? Why is it that she decided this was the direction to take her career?

We'll never fully know the answers to all the above questions; however, we know in her journey to discover herself, she reflects the current cultural concept of sexuality that has been ingrained in so many young people: sex sells. Unfortunately, the ones who are being sold into this slavery are often times those of our culture who are still growing up and developing mentally as well as physically. Miley Cyrus is a casualty of war, and the sad part is, like so many young people, she doesn't even realize what has happened to her.

WHAT ARE WE MISSING?

One of the most difficult lessons that you will encounter when it comes to either working with teens or to raising teens is the task of instilling in them a healthy self-identity. Teenagers, as you know, are constantly changing, like a river traveling through a landscape. One day they know where they're going and seem to have it all together; the next day, they're like the white water rapids of the Colorado River. They want to please, but at times they are caught in the middle of who they want to please – their friends or their parents. The truth is, if their parents are loving (notice I didn't say their parents do whatever makes them happy), even as teens they want to please both friends and parents; however, in their world, where they spend more time with their peers than their own parents, the need to fit in can take over. Clothing styles can change, hair color might be altered, and behavior can turn like a bull fresh out of the shoot. That's why you must help them find the calm when they're on that raft. You must help them see that their identity is not to be tied to their clothes, music, or even their looks.

In the creation account found in Genesis chapter 1, we read of God creating mankind in His unique image.

> *26 Then God said, "Let Us make man in Our image, according to Our likeness; and let them rule over the fish of the sea and over the birds of the sky and over the cattle and over all the earth, and over every creeping thing that creeps on the earth." 27 God created man in His own image, in the image of God He created him; male and female He created them.*

GAME PLAN

Of all the creation, humans are the only ones created in the image of God. We are unique and special because God has created an eternal soul within us, and He longs to have each soul in heaven with Him one day. His longing for us drove Him to pay the price of our sins by sending Jesus to die on the cross.

God has a reservation in heaven for those who will submit to Him through obedience to the Gospel of Jesus Christ and continue walking trusting in Him. That eternal soul will one day be in a place with no tears, no sorrow, no disappointment, and no negative image in the mind when looking in mirror. There's no marketing scheme using sexuality there, nor is there a societal expectation for our daughters to dress provocatively or for our sons to ogle women. Heaven is perfect, and God loves us so much, that He wants us to enjoy it with Him and all of our loved ones, for eternity.

While our teens are told a lot, this simple message of being created in the image of God and of God's desire for His special creation doesn't always sink into their self-perception. Teens know they're different than the rest of creation; the problem is that we're living in a world that doesn't care to focus on the unique image in which we're created. In America, our image is something we create, instead of something we reflect. We shape it by the way we dress, shows we watch, way we talk, and the behaviors we display. This modern American concept of image is not a Biblical one. The Biblical approach is that you reflect the One in whose image you were created.

When it comes to the topic of sexuality and the way we present our bodies, this identifying with God, and understanding that we are created in His image, is a matter that needs to rise to the surface. In 1 Thessalonians chapter 4, Paul instructed Christians as to how they are to behave in waiting for Christ's second coming:

> **3** *For this is the will of God, your sanctification; that is, that you abstain from sexual immorality;* **4** *that each of you knows*

THE SEXUALIZATION OF AMERICA

> *how to possess his own vessel in sanctification and honor, **5** not in lustful passion, like the Gentiles who do not know God; **6** and that no man transgress and defraud his brother in the matter because the Lord is the avenger in all these things, just as we also told you before and solemnly warned you. **7** For God has not called us for the purpose of impurity, but in sanctification.*

As Christians are waiting for Christ to come again, we need to be always aware that God desires that Christians remember we are to be different – we are set apart – we are sanctified. Specifically here, Paul tells the church members to stay away from sexual immorality, meaning anything that would get in the way of them using their bodies for honor. God's desire then, as it is today, is for our sanctification. That means in all areas.

When the teens in your life better understand their identity in the eyes of God, the rest of the teachings you will give them on the subject of purity and sexuality will make sense. When you tell them they can't wear that top, or they don't need to be moving their bodies in sexual ways to music, it will make sense to them. However, without their identity being tied to their Creator, these principles will just sound like old-fashioned rules being forced upon them again. They'll reason that the elders are out of touch with reality or that the youth minister just really hasn't made a good connection. You must instill a solid comprehension of where our identity lies in the teens you have influence over. Without it, the marketing agents continue to win, and more and more teens – including those you love, who you were thinking of when you picked up this book – will also be casualties in this war. We need more Ellas to stand up and say, "Enough is enough!"… But that won't happen if the adults in their lives fail to do their part.

GAME PLAN

CHALK TALK: WHAT'S THE GAME PLAN?

1) Quit putting sex in front of your teens on purpose!

You and I both know that, as much as we would love for Satan to never tempt our children, He will work to expose them to the sexual messages this world is using. There are absolutely zero signs to say that sexuality in selling will go away anytime soon. That being the case, you must do your part to minimize the sexual images and talk your teens are exposed to. Don't hesitate to turn off the TV or at least change the channel. Don't buy the magazines that utilize sexuality in their ads. Don't buy the video games with female characters that are dressed inappropriately. Be careful what books you buy for your children, as many authors of teen books go entirely too far in describing their characters and the activities their characters are involved in. You must not purposefully or even out of ignorance expose your children to the trash that will impact them.

2) Talk with your teens about what they're thinking and feeling when they see the ads and listen to the music.

As stated above, your teens will be exposed at some level to the sexuality that is being pushed in our culture, even with your best efforts. You will be presented with plenty of opportunities to talk with them about what they saw and the message that the marketing was really selling. I especially implore parents: please don't hesitate to ask your child how seeing the sexual images in an ad or listening to the explicit lyrics of a song makes them feel or what thoughts go through their minds. As their bodies and hormones are changing, they will be trying to figure out this whole sexuality subject. If you don't talk about it with them, they will continue to learn as much or more from other

sources – the media and their peers – as they do from you. I know you want to guide them into a healthy identity, understanding the concept of being created in God's image. To do so, you'll need to help them understand how the world is perverting something that God created as a special gift to be enjoyed within the bond of marriage.

3) Be careful of our own dress and conversations.

We know that kids listen to what we do more so than to what we say. That's why we get, and for very good reason, very disheartened when we hear of a preacher or respected member of our congregation caught in a sexual affair. Their behavior causes damage to their message of Christian living. In the same way, we as adults must be careful that our behaviors don't ruin our message to our children. The way we dress and the attention we place on looks is a reflection of our true values. Everyone wants to look nice, but there's a difference in wanting to look nice and wanting to draw the attention of others. No matter what you preach, if your teen sees you investing so much time on body image and money on clothes that are too tight or cut just right to show cleavage, then they will be impacted by that. You will inadvertently teach them a message that might be altogether different than what your words say.

This goes for dads and male adult leaders as well. When a commercial comes across during the football game that has partial nudity – i.e. underwear commercials – what do you do? How do you respond? Your children know, and they are learning how to behave from how dad handles this issue. What about the conversations your teens overhear you engaged in? Do you and your buddies inadvertently send a message that women are meant to be ogled? What we do often times can negate our message. Be careful not to "accidently" give your teens a reason not to listen to your godly advice.

CHAPTER 10

RAISE THE BAR

It was the biggest game, on the biggest stage. That's what we find in I Samuel chapter 17 when we observe the enormous man named Goliath as he taunted the army of God. He proclaimed that if the children of God could send out one man who could beat him then all of the Philistines would serve the Israelites; but if that man failed and Goliath triumphed, the Israelites would be forever in the service of the Philistines. This huge challenge led the children of God, along with King Saul, to be afraid. Because they did not place their trust in the power of God, and because they knew their own human limitations, they thought defeating Goliath was an impossible feat.

All of that changed when a certain young man, who was bringing provisions to his brothers, overheard the repetitive challenge as he came into the camp. His reaction was confident, not in himself, but in God:

> **26** *"What will be done for the man who kills this Philistine and takes away the reproach from Israel? For who is this uncircumcised Philistine, that he should taunt the armies of the living God?"*

When he posed this question of what the king would do for the man who could silence this uncircumcised Philistine, David found out that Saul would elevate him; however, that was not the major attraction. The most significant reason for David's actions was the fact that none of his Israelite brothers had enough faith in God to believe that He would provide a victory.

GAME PLAN

So David went, taking with him a sling and smooth stones that he picked up along the way. As he approached Goliath, he heard the degrading taunts and boldly replied,

> **45** *"You come to me with a sword, a spear, and a javelin, but I come to you in the name of the LORD of hosts, the God of the armies of Israel, whom you have taunted." (1 Samuel 17:45)*

David refused to bow to the expectation of the others in the Israelite army. He refused to give in to the giant. He aimed to rise to God's expectation.

God truly does expect His people to be different. He expects His children to stand up and to rise to the challenges placed before us, to be more than what this world expects. That's where we, as a culture, have failed young people today. We've failed them in the sense that we have set the bar of expectations so low that we're happy when teens wake up on time, brush their teeth, and make their beds – but that is not what the expectations in America used to be for this young group.

Have you ever observed someone use a simple stick and a tap on the leg to move massive, but well-trained, elephants? The training for this behavior begins by attaching a chain to the back right leg of a baby elephant. The other end of the chain is connected to an immovable object such as a tree. As the baby elephant tries to move away, pulling with all the might it can muster, it feels the restriction. Over time, the baby elephant realizes it can't get away.

As the elephant ages it progresses into another portion of training. The trainers decrease the strength of the chain and of the immovable object. However, every time the elephant pulls, its mind registers, "I've got something tied around my back right leg. I can't get away." As the training concludes, a one-ton animal with a piece of twine tied around its back leg is tethered to a small stick hammered into the ground. While the large elephant, by all measure, is fully capable of snapping the small stick, it doesn't – because the elephant has been convinced it can't.

As a society, we have tied the leg of today's teens, conditioning them to believe that they can't do much, so there's no reason to try. Our society has failed them, by lowering expectations.

RAISE THE BAR

Does the name David Farragut sound familiar? Farragut was raised in Tennessee, and by the age of 9, was a midshipman in the United States Navy. By his early 20s he had reached a high level in the military, and he would eventually become the very first rear admiral of the United States Navy. Who at the age of 9 is a midshipman today? Who would ever dream of placing a young 20-year old in a similar position? In our society we would never dream of that. That's not because society has always been this way. It's because as America aged, we decided to lower the expectations on teens, assuming they could not accomplish what teens in days gone by had accomplished.

Admiral David Farragut

GOD'S BAR IN SOCIETY

In the book of 1 Samuel chapter 8, we understand that Samuel is older in age, selected by God as both a prophet and judge. He's a leader of the children of Israel, but due to his old age, he appoints his two sons, Joel and Abijah, to take his place. The only problem with this major appointment is,

> 3 *"His sons, however, did not walk in his ways, but turned aside after dishonest gain, and took bribes and perverted justice."*

Who would want to follow that? Who wants to follow two individuals that don't even look at justice as something that is to be elevated and followed after? The elders of the children of Israel came to the conclusion that they did not, and they demanded a king, making them like every other nation.

Now, obviously, you can imagine Samuel's great disappointment, his great hurt, as if he's been rejected himself. And so he goes and inquires of God, and God replies,

> 7 *"Listen to the voice of the people in regard to all that they say to you, for they have not rejected you, but they have rejected Me from being king over them." (1 Samuel 8:7)*

GAME PLAN

Give us a king. With this desire to be just like others around them, the children of God began to encounter all kinds of turmoil – resulting in death, captivity, confusion, and despair. Like children, they only saw what they wanted in the moment, not being able to, or else not taking the time, to consider the consequences of their decision.

As we progress from infants to elderly, we go through stages. During some stages, we may care more about our parents; during others, we may care more about friends. But in reality, when we become teenagers, there are a few fundamental concepts that are crucial to us. **First and foremost, teenagers don't like to be made fun of.** Now, I realize they may laugh along with each other, but deep down they don't want to be made fun of. **Also, teenagers don't want to be isolated from the group, and they don't want to be made to feel like they're not good enough.** One of the most hurtful things today's teens encounter is when they know their friends are getting together to do something, but they aren't included. To be left out hurts, and for some reason it seems to hurt more as a teenager than as an adult.

By Def·i·ni·tion

ex·pec·ta·tion —n
the act or state of looking forward or anticipating.

So what's the usual response? Well, they attempt to fit in with the expectations. Every group has expectations, even if they are not spoken outright. It's not as if anyone will declare that you have to wear this pair of jeans, or you must wear that shirt, or your hair needs to be styled in this way or with that color. It's not an articulated thing; it's an unspoken thing learned through observations. It's heard in the language used, looks given, conversations held, and in the attitudes and behaviors of peers.

Well, what happens when young people have expectations within one group that don't line up with their other groups? Maybe a church youth group has expectations, but those expectations don't line up with school friends. Possibly those expectations don't line up with another group, such as a sports team. What happens when a teenager finds herself in the middle of all these social circles, but the expectations are different within each of them? Like many teenagers today, she's tempted to become a chameleon, changing to blend with whatever group she's with at that particular time. If the truth be told, such behavior is a defense mechanism for a chameleon – just as it is for a teen. The chameleon will change to fit its surroundings, so a predator can't come and pick it out of the forest or the desert. For the teen, it's not so much a predator in the desert she's afraid of, but the social predators who might isolate her, ridicule her, and influence others not to accept her.

When the group says you're supposed to be involved in a particular activity, that teenager follows. When the group says this is the way you talk, the teenager who might never talk that way around his church youth group friends will possibly change, just to fit in. Most teens will do almost anything to avoid being placed on an island of loneliness. It's a common fear when we go through the teen years, and we will do whatever it takes to stay off of that isolated island, even if it means compromising in certain areas of life.

One of the areas that teenagers often struggle with is the language that flows from their mouths. In Ephesians chapter 4, the apostle Paul makes it very clear that what we say and what comes out of our mouth does matter, when he says,

> **29** *"Let no unwholesome word proceed from your mouth."*

Did Paul mean that we can actually speak unwholesome words? We most definitely can! Unwholesome words can include language that hurts others, language that is not considered holy, and language that is not considered righteous. As Christians, those words ought not to come from us. But many will attempt to justify such language when the captain of the football team is telling a joke in the locker room, or when they've become frustrated on the field- at that point, how could Paul have meant for this passage to pertain to them?! *(I hope you hear the sarcasm.)*

Paul continues to write in the book of Ephesians chapter 5,

> **4** *"and there must be no filthiness and silly talk, or coarse jesting, which are not fitting, but rather giving of thanks."*

The last time I checked, what comes out of our mouths comes from within us. Therefore, if I'm spouting off filthiness, it has to come from

somewhere. If I'm getting involved with coarse jesting or these jokes that I shouldn't be telling or laughing along with, my heart is not, in that moment, concerned with reaching for God's expectations. When this occurs, such behavior demonstrates a heart that has been heavily influenced by the world's expectations. As Christians, we cannot let society drive our lives, not even in regard to what comes out of our mouth. If you don't want the teens in your life to talk a certain way, they must not live in an environment that uses cuss words or is involved in filthiness of talk.

When it comes to the subject of the language used, one of the peaks of influence is, again, the media. As referenced in a previous chapter, in July of 2010, the U.S. Second Circuit Court of Appeals handed down its ruling in the case of *Fox v. FCC*. To summarize the dispute, the FCC (Federal Communications Commission) exercised its right to enforce broadcast decency laws. Fox charged that their freedoms were being restricted and thus sought to end these broad laws. In a landmark conclusion, the court ruled the FCC could not restrict the "fleeting expletives" to the late night hours when most children were not watching.

With this ruling, the flood gates of "expression" and "freedom speech" were opened and the waters are now freely flowing into nearly every home in America. In a recent study conducted by the Parents Television Council comparing the use of expletives in 2005 with those used in 2010, they discovered:

- The use of profanity in prime-time broadcast programming increased 69.3 percent from 2005 to 2010.
- The greatest increase in the use of the harshest profanities occurred in the 8:00 ET time period – commonly thought of as the "family hour".
- The use of the bleeped or muted f-word increased 2,409 percent between 2005 and 2010.
- The use of the bleeped or muted s-word increased 281 percent from 2005 to 2010.[1]

With this strong influence in the lives of many teens, it should not surprise us then that Dr. Timothy Jay, a leading expert in research on cussing in society, reveals that teens are swearing on average, 80-90 times each day. His studies go on to reveal that

- 75% of high school students report hearing "adult language" in school settings.
- 74% of 18 to 34 year olds admit to swearing in public.
- Elementary school teachers report children are using more offensive language at school than they have in the past.[2]

While we might be tempted to place the entirety of the blame on outlets such as the media, studies show that parents are the number one influence in the child's life when it comes to this issue. When children and teens hear their parents using choice words, they assume the words must be acceptable to use themselves. Granted, they don't always know what the words mean, but that doesn't stop a child from repeating what he's heard.

Unfortunately, in a world driven by the Internet, what they hear in the school hallways or on the television is not the only threat to our teens. Many of you are familiar with social networking sites such as Facebook; however, you might not be aware that

- 47% of users have profanity on their Facebook wall.
- 80% of users who have profanity on their Facebook wall have at least one post or comment with profanity from a friend.
- 56% of the posts with profanity on a user's Facebook wall come from friends.
- The most common profane word is derivations of the f-word.
- The second most common profane word is derivations of the s-word.
- B***h is a distant third.[3]

God's bar of expectations is set high. When it comes to the issue of language, we not only must decide if we're going to live by God's expectations; we must help the teens in our life avoid fitting the "cookie-cutter" mold of this society. Individuals in the book of I Samuel wanted to

GAME PLAN

become like everyone else. However, in becoming like everyone else, there were consequences, as can clearly be seen in I Samuel 8:10-21, in what I call the "He will" passages:

> *He will take your sons and daughters*
> *He will take your land*
> *He will bring your sons into battle*

All the "He will" statements declare that there is a problem when people follow what society teaches instead of what God instructs. That's really what I Peter 2:9-12 is all about as well: God has called us to be different, living as aliens and strangers in a world in which we don't belong. The question is this: have you become so comfortable here on earth that you blend right in like the chameleon and have stopped living for heaven?

GOD'S BAR IN THE FAMILY

When you really read the Bible to determine God's general expectations of families, you begin to understand that young people fit into that family much the same way that fathers do and much the same way that mothers do. As a matter of fact, when we look at the book of Ephesians, a very common passage comes to our minds about the way that a husband and a wife should respond to one another. It's a beautiful passage in which Paul told the church as a whole to be in subjection to each other, even as he summarized the way that moms and dads, husbands and wives, should treat each other. He proceeded to specifically detail how wives should respond to their husbands and how husbands should respond to their wives. He even wrote in verse 22,

> *"Wives, be subject to your own husbands as to the Lord; for the husband is the head of the wife, as Christ also is the head of the church, he himself being the savior of the body."*

Paul proceeded to write in verse 25,

> *"Husbands, love your wives just as Christ also loved the church and gave himself up for her."*

You and I have heard sermon after sermon; we've studied, I'm sure, in Bible class after Bible class the reality that God has expectations for husbands and wives. And you notice that within that writing, nowhere does it say that the wife is supposed to respond to the husband because the husband deserves it nor the husband respond to the wife because she deserves it. I mean, let's face it. If we responded to people because they deserved it, how nice would we really be to some of the people who we come in contact with? If the way that we are supposed to act is solely based upon what that person deserves or doesn't deserve, then think about it: what do you deserve from others? What do I deserve? If the way my parents respond to me, or in particular the way my wife responds to me, is based upon whether or not I'm a perfect man or whether or not I always do what I'm supposed to do and treat her as I'm supposed to treat her, how would you honestly think she would respond to me?

Interestingly though, the Bible never tells wives to be subject to their husbands because husbands deserve that. And the Bible never says husbands must love their wives as Christ loved the church because wives are perfect and deserving. You see, in the family unit, God's expectation is that you will act in the way that He says, not because the other person deserves it but because you respect His command to do so.

Think about how society regards teenagers within the family: When Mom says, "Take out the trash," society says the normal teenage response is, "Do I have to?" If Mom says, "Clean your room," we think nothing is odd when we hear, "Oh, mom- I did it last week." Dad says, "Son, get out and mow the yard," and what happens? Well, he may hear back, "Yes, sir", but his son only does it kicking and screaming the whole way, like a child who never grew up to realize that they're supposed to respond differently to their parents.

You see, it's within this same passage of Ephesians that we see a shift out of chapter 5 into chapter 6, where the Bible says,

GAME PLAN

> *1 "Children obey your parents in the Lord, for this is right.
> 2 Honor your father and mother, which is the first commandment with a promise so that it may be well with you and that you may live long on the earth."*

Obey and honor. That's God's expectation? Many say, "I've got it. I understand what obey means. That means when I'm told to do something, I just do it." Well, that's a part of obedience. But notice he takes it beyond blind obedience to "honor your parents". You see, a child who will follow the letter of the law doesn't necessarily honor his parents. But a child who, for the right reasons, and with the right attitude and motivation, does what his parents tell him to do? That child honors his parents.

Have you ever known someone that may have done what their parents said but bad-mouthed their parents the whole time? Most likely you have; we've all been teenagers, and we understand some of that dynamic and thought pattern. Our understanding of it doesn't make it right, nor does it mean that such behavior stems from God. Society may say it's normal to bad-mouth a parent or authority figure who told you to do something, because no one likes authority. But that's not what God says; He simply says for children to obey and honor their parents.

Have you ever thought about what it means to honor? You know, I could give you a dictionary definition, but I would much rather give you an object lesson.

If you have ever had the opportunity to visit Washington, D.C., you may have visited the Tomb of the Unknown Soldier. Keeping watch over this monument on a 24/7 basis is the Society of the Honor Guard - Tomb of the Unknown Soldier. Whenever I have visited the Tomb, I have always been awed by the seriousness of the moment, and how professional the soldier is. But I never really realized what the guard does, why he does it, and the commitment that he makes in accepting a post at the Tomb of the Unknown Soldier.

You see, not just anybody can serve in the "Old Guard", as it's referred to. An individual has to be of a certain physical caliber – between 5 feet 11 inches and 6 feet 2 inches, and with a waist of no more than 30 inches (I guess that would eliminate some of us!). Along with the physical aspect,

RAISE THE BAR

there is a commitment aspect that requires true dedication. The first six months of service are spent in rigorous training; these guards must know the names and interment locations of the many prominent figures buried in Arlington National Cemetery. They will learn of those who sacrificed their life during World War II, as well as individuals who sacrificed and fought valiantly in Vietnam and the Civil War and World War I and the Korean War.

Guards will also learn that how they dress on-shift matters: their gun must be polished, their shoes must be spotless, and their medals, belt and hat must be worn in just the right way and place. Anything less is considered disrespectful and dishonorable. It takes five hours just for an individual to prepare to stand guard, and they stand guard only for 30-minute to one-hour intervals, depending on the season. This happens 365 days a year, rain or shine, day or night. You will always find a guard posted at the Tomb of the Unknown Soldier, to honor those who have given their lives in service.

As they continue in their training, the guards learn that everything they do is to be precisely executed, since each step, quite literally, is considered significant. When walking the area in front of the tomb, the guard will take 21 steps from one end to the next, representing a 21-gun salute, which is the highest honor that an individual can receive after sacrificing his or her life in military service. The guard will then pause 21 seconds before turning 90 degrees due east, where he

The Sentinel's Creed

My dedication to this sacred duty is total and whole-hearted.

In the responsibility bestowed on me never will I falter.

And with dignity and perseverance my standard will remain perfection.

Through the years of diligence and praise and the discomfort of the elements, I will walk my tour in humble reverence to the best of my ability. It is he who commands the respect I protect, his bravery that made us so proud.

Surrounded by well meaning crowds by day, alone in the thoughtful peace of night, this soldier will in honored glory rest under my eternal vigilance.[4]

will again pause for 21 seconds. These turns and pauses are repeated until he is facing north, when he steps out to again begin his walk.

If you observe the process, you'll also notice that the guard switches the shoulder on which the gun is carried, symbolizing his commitment to stand between the tomb and any threat.[5] He stands prepared to defend all of those who have given their life or gone missing in battle.

That is what honor truly means.

You see, God's expectations in the family are not for the faint of heart. They're not always easy. There may be times that as adults, we do mess up by saying some things we shouldn't say or responding in ways we shouldn't respond. But that goes all the way back to how God expects me to respond to people in my family – not always in the way they deserve, but in the way He commands, because I love Him. Young people need to realize too, that dad may not always deserve honor and respect. However, as a Christian teenager, they ought not to respond to dad respectfully and honorably only when he deserves it, but always. When we act in this way, we show God and those around us that we love Him. Through this level of obedience, we demonstrate that we have died, been buried, and been resurrected to walk in newness of life, having our sins washed away through the waters of baptism. We are no longer walking as the old self. And when we no longer walk as the old self, we act differently even within the family.

GOD'S BAR IN THE CHURCH

One of the biggest mistakes we make in the religious world is telling teenagers that they aren't the Church of today. I know we don't say it in those exact words, but we tell them through our prayers and even in sermons – they are the Church of tomorrow. Inadvertently, we are teaching them that they don't have to be serious today, because their time is coming in the future, when they will have to pick up the reins and lead. The problem with this way of thinking is that if they have obeyed the Gospel of Jesus Christ according to the Bible, they are just as much a part of the Church of today as you and I are. In the Bible, we read,

> *"And the Lord was adding to their number day by day those who were being saved." (Acts 2:47)*

Notice that the Bible doesn't classify some New Testament Christians as partial members of the body of Christ, or that the Lord added the adults but not the teenagers. Without thinking about it, when we say they are the "Church of Tomorrow" we give teens an excuse not be more serious not only about their relationship with Jesus Christ, but also about the active role they must play in the local congregation if the body of Christ – the Church - is going to function in a healthy manner.

We read in 1 Corinthians chapter 12,

> **14** *For the body is not one member, but many.* **15** *If the foot says, "Because I am not a hand, I am not a part of the body," it is not for this reason any the less a part of the body.* **16** *And if the ear says, "Because I am not an eye, I am not a part of the body," it is not for this reason any the less a part of the body.* **17** *If the whole body were an eye, where would the hearing be? If the whole were hearing, where would the sense of smell be?* **18** *But now God has placed the members, each one of them, in the body, just as He desired.*

Just as the church in Corinth needed these words as they were struggling with their misunderstanding of spiritual gifts, we need these words as we struggle with understanding that God has given every New Testament Christian different abilities and that He really expects each of us to function in the Church based upon His will and not ours. Paul's desire, as he was inspired by the Holy Spirit, was to bring the Christians in Corinth to the understanding that no matter how small a gift they might have had, the overall function of the body could not happen without everyone working together to fulfill their part.

When you consider the human body, this spiritual principle is very obvious. A human hair seems very simple. However, when you split one single strand open and begin to understand the complex workings on the microscopic level you begin to comprehend just how important those small parts and the processes they fulfill are to the overall health of the single strand of hair.

GAME PLAN

Our bones are the same. We have some long bones, such as in the leg, and some that are short, like the bones of the wrist; each fulfills a very important purpose. Additionally, there is diversity and a necessary cooperation that happens inside each and every bone, as a very hard, inorganic material called hydroxylapatite works in conjunction with a tough, fibrous organic material called collagen to add just the right amount of strength and flexibility. If a bone has too much hydroxylapatite, an individual will have very brittle bones. If there is too much collagen, the bones are easily bent – resulting in multiple breaks.

Along with the components making the strength and flexibility of bones possible, there are also smaller parts called osteoblasts and osteoclasts that must be present if the bones are going to last very long. The osteoblasts are cells that are responsible for continuous regeneration of bone. In other words, they make bone. If something is making bone, it would then make sense that another cell would be continually breaking down bone. That's where the osteoclasts come in. The balance between these two cells is crucial to the health of the overall bone, and thus to the overall body.

The importance of each and every body part is also well-demonstrated when looking at the small portion of the brain called the hypothalamus. It's this small part of your brain that kicks in when you are faced with extremely cold conditions, creating involuntary responses such as shivering to keep the body warm. If your body gets cold enough, the hypothalamus will send signals to the body in order to decrease the blood flow to your feet, hands and surface skin. Finally, should the exposure to cold be extreme and prolonged, the hypothalamus will actually send signals to your body to begin shutting down organs that aren't immediately needed for your life to be sustained over a short time.

We know these smaller, seemingly insignificant parts of our body are important for life; however, if we could choose which part of the body we would want to be, how many of us would choose to be the inside working of the hair or the inward components of the bone? Spiritually speaking, this is exactly what the church in Corinth was struggling with. They knew their "smaller gifts" were needed, but there was a push to be up in front of the crowds with a gift that would bring recognition, such as speaking in tongues. Paul reminded them,

RAISE THE BAR

> *22 On the contrary, it is much truer that the members of the body which seem to be weaker are necessary; 23 and those members of the body which we deem less honorable, on these we bestow more abundant honor, and our less presentable members become much more presentable, 24 whereas our more presentable members have no need of it. But God has so composed the body, giving more abundant honor to that member which lacked, 25 so that there may be no division in the body, but that the members may have the same care for one another. (1 Corinthians 12)*

Understanding that teenagers are just as much a part of the body of Christ as adults are, and that God has placed them in the body where He wills, will help us as we teach them to see the bar that is set for them in the Church. God really expects more of teens than for them to sit on the back row and text message one another during worship service. He really expects more than for them to sit through and endure a Sunday morning class as they fight against falling asleep because they stayed out entirely too late on Saturday night. He has placed each one of us in the body and we have a responsibility. If I am not doing my part, the body suffers as others must cover tasks that I can and should be doing. In the same way, when teenagers who are New Testament Christians are continually told they can get serious in the future about being a part of the body, we are not only hurting their understanding of what the Church is, but we are teaching them a message that is against the Word of God.

Returning to the biggest stage in 1 Samuel 17, we remember that those around David were reacting out of fear and remaining in their state of complacency. David however, acted faithfully, and with complete confidence in God, decided he would step up to the challenge. Using any human logic, David should have never defeated the much larger, better equipped, professional soldier Goliath. Aren't you glad that David didn't use human logic? Instead he knew that if he simply walked into the battle trusting in God victory would be provided. While others around him acted as if they were elephants with chains around their back right legs, David made a commitment to strive for what was right in God's eyes. That's exactly what we want for each of our teens.

GAME PLAN

CHALK TALK: WHAT'S THE GAME PLAN?

1) Set the right example.

It's very easy to get frustrated when we hear teens cussing and talking in profane ways; however, we must remember that our children will repeat what they hear. Make sure they aren't hearing the cuss words and the profanities from you. There will be plenty of people in the world who will quickly introduce them to all kinds of phrases. If you hear your child say one of them, stop then and make sure they understand what they've just said. Show them how ignorant it is, and most importantly bring them back to the Bible, explaining to them God's will for their tongue.

2) As a family, take on a task in your local congregation and let your teens lead it.

Maybe it's a food drive or collecting medical supplies for a missionary that would serve as the spark your teen needs to understand her importance in the body. Dads, take the reins and show your sons how to organize and how to communicate with the elders. Ask for a meeting with the leadership of the Church, and have your teen come into that meeting with notes and a plan to share with them. Moms, show your children how to follow through on the small details. You will be amazed at what they will learn.

3) Have chores in your family for your children.

There are plenty of people who are quick to tell parents they should "let kids be kids," meaning don't give them work to do rather let them play. While I'm all for creative playing to help develop the brain, we also need to teach children from the youngest ages that they are a part of the family and that means that they add to the family. By giving

RAISE THE BAR

your children chores, you will teach them that they are important to the family and that responsibility is expected. Don't cheat them of this valuable lesson.

PRACTICE DRILLS

Now that you've studied the opponent's schemes and considered what you can do in helping your teen have a winning *Game Plan*, consider some of these very real and tough decisions that young people must make. Don't just read the words. I encourage you to read the scenario first and pause, asking yourself what you would tell your teen if they were in the same predicament. Once you've processed the scenario, consider the possible responses – weigh them all against the teaching found within the Bible – and develop a *Game Plan* that you can use to teach the teen in your life. I encourage you, as their parents and spiritual mentors, discuss these and other subjects with your young people now, before they possibly encounter them. The goal is not to simply sit back and be reactionary. Rather, the idea is to be proactive and involved in helping teens implement the *Game Plan*.

Practice Drill #1 — Anger

Frank's younger brother, Charlie, has done it again! He has his own clothes, but for some reason, Charlie thinks he needs to sneak into Frank's room and take his favorite sweater. Since Frank goes to school earlier than Charlie, he doesn't notice it until the next day. He's getting ready for school and goes looking for the sweater, only to discover that it's not there. He is burning mad, but…what should he do?

Option 1: Go into Charlie's room and start yelling at him.

Positive: Charlie gets the message that Frank's not going to put up with this anymore.

Negative: A big yelling match happens, and Frank and Charlie's relationship suffers.

Option 2: Frank tells his parents about the sweater and tells Charlie to just ask first next time.

Positive: Charlie's respect for Frank increases and their parents are aware that Frank has asked Charlie nicely not to do this again.

PRACTICE DRILLS

Negative: Charlie may not get the message to show more respect toward Frank by not taking his clothes without asking.

Option 3: Go into Charlie's room and start taking his clothes in a rage.

Positive: Frank gets back at him, and Charlie gets to feel what it's like to have his clothes taken.

Negative: It will probably end up in a big fight, and they will both get in big trouble.

Bible:

1. James 1:19-20 – "This you know, my beloved brethren. But everyone must be quick to hear, slow to speak and slow to anger; for the anger of man does not achieve the righteousness of God."

2. Proverbs 15:1 – "A soft answer turns away wrath, but a harsh word stirs up anger."

3. Proverbs 19: 11 – "A man's discretion makes him slow to anger, and it is his glory to overlook a transgression."

4. 1 Peter 4: 8 – "Above all, keep fervent in your love for one another, because love covers a multitude of sins."

What should Frank do?

The dreaded "Sweater Swipe"! It's Frank's nightmare come true. He loves that sweater, and he gets so angry when Charlie thinks it's ok to just take it. However, going into Charlie's room and yelling at him won't solve anything; it will only show that Frank is mad. If he goes in and starts taking Charlie's clothes just to prove a point, then his actions are no better than Charlie's. Frank opens his Bible and reads the above passages about being slow to anger and love covering a bunch of sins.

What should he do? Option 2 is the only real response that will accomplish what Frank wants, a long-term fix to the problem. Charlie must know he can't do this again, but Frank needs to show him love, and show his parents that he is mature enough to solve problems without yelling and fighting.

GAME PLAN

Practice Drill #2 — Fitting In

Andrew recently transferred schools, and although he doesn't want to admit that he cares so much, he really wants to fit in. He meets a new group of guys he thinks will be good for his image and he enjoys hanging out with them. The only problem is the crude language they use, which doesn't match Andrew's lifestyle. Every time they say certain words (and it happens more often than he'd like to admit), he cringes inside. He is torn about what to do.

Option 1: Ignore the language.

Positive: He doesn't have to be embarrassed by confronting the situation and feeling foolish.

Negative: He is not facing a problem head on, which may cause more problems in the future.

Option 2: Start ignoring this group, and find another group of friends to hang out with.

Positive: He will remove himself from the language, which makes him so uncomfortable.

Negative: He didn't really deal with the situation.

Option 3: Explain to his new friends that he really enjoys hanging out with them, but their language is not pleasing to God, and is making him uncomfortable.

Positive: He is being honest; as they say, "honesty is the best policy".

Negative: His new friends may shun him, and then he'll really feel like he doesn't fit in.

Bible:

1. 1 Corinthians 15: 33 - "Do not be deceived: Bad company corrupts good morals."

PRACTICE DRILLS

2. Ephesians 5:8 – "for you were formerly darkness, but now you are Light in the Lord; walk as children of Light."

3. 1 John 1: 5-6 – "This is the message we have heard from Him and announce to you, that God is Light, and in Him there is no darkness at all. If we say that we have fellowship with Him and yet walk in the darkness, we lie and do not practice the truth;"

4. Ephesians 4:29 – "Let no unwholesome word proceed from your mouth, but only such a word as is good for edification according to the need of the moment, so that it will give grace to those who hear."

5. Ephesians 5:4 – "and there must be no filthiness and silly talk, or coarse jesting, which are not fitting, but rather giving of thanks."

What should Andrew do?

Compromising morals and values for the purpose of fitting in is always a bad idea, but Andrew's already in the group. It's good that he wants out because, as a Christian, his new friends' lifestyle is not matching his walk. Option 1 is out of the question. To continue on as if nothing is wrong only opens Andrew up to be influenced to talk the same way. It's easy to get pulled down if you hang around sin. Option 3 is the best option. Andrew wants these guys to change. He's got to care about them enough to say something. Maybe they will respect him, and he can be a great influence. If not, Option 2 is the next step he must take. It's better to surround yourself with those walking in the Light just as you are.

GAME PLAN

Practice Drill #3 — Handling Bullies

Matthew has had some trouble with one of the older guys in his neighborhood, Joey. Every time Matthew walks down the street and comes across him, Joey always bullies him by pushing, punching, and taking his money. Joey has even started causing trouble in school for Matthew. Matthew's getting really tired of this, but what should he do?

Option 1: Fight back against Joey.
Positive: Joey will know that Matthew is going to stand up for himself.
Negative: Joey could decide to really beat him up.

Option 2: Tell parents about the problem.
Positive: Dad gets involved and stops the bullying.
Negative: Matthew's friends will learn that his daddy had to save him; his peers might make fun.

Option 3: Talk with Joey about stopping. If he doesn't stop – involve the police.
Positive: Maybe the problem could be solved without fighting.
Negative: Joey might not respond and will then come after Matthew even more.

Bible:

1. Matthew 5: 38-39 – "You have heard that it was said, 'An eye for an eye and a tooth for a tooth.' But I tell you not to resist an evil person. But whoever slaps you on your right cheek, turn the other to him also."

2. Matthew 5: 16 – "Let your light so shine before men, that they may see your good works and glorify your Father in heaven."

3. Romans 13: 1-3 – "Let every person be subject to the governing authorities. For there is no authority except from God, and those that exist have been instituted by God. Therefore whoever resists the authorities resists what God

PRACTICE DRILLS

has appointed, and those who resist will incur judgment. For rulers are not a terror to good conduct, but to bad. Would you have no fear of the one who is in authority? Then do what is good, and you will receive his approval,"

4. 1 Thessalonians 5: 15 – "See that no one repays another with evil for evil, but always seek after that which is good for one another and for all people."

What should Matthew do?

Let's say Matthew hits Joey next time he bullies him. Is Joey going to get even more mad and hit Matthew harder? Should Matthew make this his first response? Based upon the Bible, the answer would be "NO". Option 2 would be a good response. As Matthew's parents, they need to know when he's having difficulties so they can help. God expects Matthew's parents to raise him according to the Word of God even when he encounters bullies. Option 3 is one that should definitely be done if the bullying is serious. The Bible allows us to be protected by the police, and there's nothing wrong with Matthew and his parents going to the police to let them know what's going on. Matthew should then tell Joey that he is not afraid of him and ask him why he feels the need to bully. He should also tell him that if he ever tries to bully him again the police are already aware of the situation and action will be taken.

GAME PLAN

Practice Drill #4 — Integrity

Brock's chemistry teacher assigned some massive homework on Friday, but with Brock's action-packed weekend, the homework didn't even get touched. Now it's Monday. He goes to school early, thinking he can get at least some of it done before first period. As he's sitting in homeroom, Ally shows up with all of it done. She offers to let him "look" at it. What should he do?

Option 1: Have a "look"!

Positive: Brock gets the homework done and moves on with life.

Negative: It's cheating! If he gets caught, it's a Big Fat Zero. Most importantly, God will know.

Option 2: Do his own work really quick, then take Ally's to "look at" – changing answers as needed.

Positive: It's done and he gets the grade.

Negative: He might have done his own work, but it's still cheating if he copies her answers. Result – Big Fat Zero for dishonesty. Oh yeah, and God knows too!

Option 3: Tell Ally, "Thanks, but no thanks."

Positive: Brock gets the grade he deserves while learning to be better prepared next time. Plus, Ally sees Brock as an honest guy (A Big Positive!).

Negative: Brock takes the risk of not getting it done and getting a bad grade.

Bible:

1. John 8: 44 – "You are of your father the devil, and you want to do the desires of your father. He was a murderer from the beginning, and does not stand in the truth because there is no truth in him. Whenever he speaks a lie, he speaks from his own nature, for he is a liar and the father of lies."

2. Ephesians 4: 28 – "Let him who stole steal no longer, but rather let him labor, working with his hands what is good, that he may have something to give him who has need."

3. Revelation 21: 8 – "But the cowardly, unbelieving, abominable, murderers, sexually immoral, sorcerers, idolaters, and all liars shall have their part in the lake which burns with fire and brimstone, which is the second death."

4. Luke 16: 10 – "One who is faithful in a very little is also faithful in much, and one who is dishonest in a very little is also dishonest in much."

What should Brock do?

This one is pretty easy! Option 3 is the only one that allows Brock to obey the teachings found within the Bible regarding lying and stealing. The truth is, it would be easy for him to "borrow" Ally's homework answers, and the teacher would probably never even find out about it… but Brock's not living his life only concerned with whether the teacher finds out about it. He's concerned with pleasing God, and he knows that God will see if he copies from Ally's homework.

What should he do? Take responsibility for his actions. He can get as much done as time will allow in homeroom, but he should not bend his morals by cheating. This is one of those times that Brock has to take what's coming his way. Life lesson learned!

GAME PLAN

Practice Drill #5 — Modesty

Donna's question: "What am I going to wear?" You see, summer is coming up, and a big group of her friends is planning a trip to the beach. She needs to get a swimsuit but doesn't really know which one to get. She knows whatever she gets, she wants it look pretty and cool. All the other girls have already talked about their bikinis, and Donna knows that if she doesn't have one, it will be noticed. What's she going to do?

Option 1: Get the bikini – everyone else will have one.
Positive: Josh will definitely notice her, and so will all the other guys. She loves the attention, and it will help her fit in with the rest of the girls.
Negative: That's a lot of skin showing. She wouldn't walk around in her underwear, which covers probably more than the bikini will. She is a stumbling block for the boys to be pure in their minds and thinking.

Option 2: Don't get the bikini – a modest one-piece with a cover works just fine.
Positive: She still gets to enjoy the sun but doesn't feel so self-conscious about her body. Plus, with the cover, the guys' minds might not wonder and go to impure thoughts.
Negative: The rest of the girls will definitely notice, and she will be the talk. She probably won't get as much attention from the guys, which means she might feel left out at times.

Option 3: Opt for the cool and trendy board shorts with a swim shirt.
Positive: Less sunburn! Seriously – she doesn't have to worry about causing her guy friends to lust. It will then simply be about the fun of the beach trip, not about what she is wearing – or not wearing.
Negative: She won't get the attention from the guys because of the skin she is showing. Also, she will look different than the rest of the girls, so she might get talked about some.

PRACTICE DRILLS

Bible:

5. Matthew 5:14 – "You are the light of the world. A city that is set on a hill cannot be hidden."

6. I Timothy 2:9-10 – "in like manner also, that the women adorn themselves in modest apparel, with propriety and moderation, not with braided hair or gold or pearls or costly clothing, but, which is proper for women professing godliness, with good works."

7. I Thessalonians 4:3-8 – "For this is the will of God, your sanctification: that you should abstain from sexual immorality; that each of you should know how to possess his own vessel in sanctification and honor, not in passion of lust, like the Gentiles who do not know God…Therefore he who rejects this does not reject man, but God, who has also given us His Holy Spirit."

8. Romans 13:13-14 – "Let us behave properly as in the day, not in carousing and drunkenness, not in sexual promiscuity and sensuality, not in strife and jealousy. But put on the Lord Jesus Christ, and make no provision for the flesh in regard to its lusts."

9. I Peter 2:9-12 – "But you are a chosen generation, a royal priesthood, a holy nation, His own special people, that you may proclaim the praises of Him who called you out of darkness into His marvelous light"

What Will Donna Do?

Taking into consideration what the Bible says about lust, sexual immorality and sensuality – and adding how teen boys are wired to be attracted by sight so strongly – Donna throws out Option 1. After looking at the Bible, she figures that Option 2 would be OK, but she concludes that Option 3 is probably the safest response. She will still get to swim and hang out with the others, but she is not going to run the risk of causing someone to sin because of the way she is dressed. Plus, she is noticed for her difference, which gives her a chance to share the reason she chose to dress differently – Jesus.

GAME PLAN

Practice Drill #6 — Obedience to Parents

Michael thinks he has great parents and doesn't usually have a problem with the guidelines and rules they set before him. He knows they love him and are looking out for his best interest…but lately, it feels like they are making all kinds of strict and crazy rules. He tries to remind himself that his parents just want what's best for him, but he is angry that they don't appear to trust him as much as they used to, and he is not sure why. He is faced with the dilemma of what to do.

Option 1: Go against his parents' rules.

Positive: He still gets to do what he believes is fair and appropriate for his life.

Negative: He will be disobeying his parents, and if they find out it might destroy their trust in him.

Option 2: Obey his parents' new rules.

Positive: His relationship with his parents won't be damaged and they will be respect him more because he did what they told him.

Negative: He will miss out on a lot of things he wants to do.

Option 3: Talk to his parents to find out why they have become stricter.

Positive: He will learn what is really going on and have a better understanding of the situation.

Negative: He may not like his parents' answer.

Bible:

1. Ephesians 6: 1-3 – "Children, obey your parents in the Lord, for this is right. HONOR YOUR FATHER AND MOTHER (which is the first commandment with a promise), SO THAT IT MAY BE WELL WITH YOU, AND THAT YOU MAY LIVE LONG ON THE EARTH."

2. Proverbs 6: 20 – "My son, observe the commandment of your father and do not forsake the teaching of your mother;"

PRACTICE DRILLS

3. Colossians 3: 20 – "Children, be obedient to your parents in all things, for this is well-pleasing to the Lord."

4. Ephesians 6:4 – "Fathers, do not provoke your children to anger, but bring them up in the discipline and instruction of the Lord."

What should Michael do?

While Michael definitely wants his parents to lighten up some on their rules, he also knows they love him and want what's best for him. He can be mad and angry, but if he's going to be pleasing to God, he's got to be obedient to his parents. Therefore, Option 1 is out of the question. Option 2 must happen, even if Michael doesn't understand; however, Option 3 would probably help the situation a lot. A good, healthy, and respectful conversation would probably be a benefit for both Michael and his parents.

GAME PLAN

Practice Drill #7 — Party

David really likes Sharon. In his eyes, she's the cream of the crop. He knows she's going to be at an upcoming party, and David knows this is his chance to spend some time around her. He shows up, but notices this is not the type of party he's used to. There's alcohol, marijuana, and ecstasy being passed around like candy. As soon as he walked through the door, the reality of the situation was clear... but he really wants to spend time with Sharon. What should he do?

Option 1 Leave the party.

Positive: By leaving, David avoids temptation and does not sin.

Negative: He doesn't get to spend time with Sharon, and may face rejection from friends.

Option 2: Stay, but don't use alcohol and/or drugs.

Positive: He gets to spend time with Sharon, and he can be a positive example for his friends, who might follow his example.

Negative: If the party is busted, David's in trouble. Also, the secondhand smoke isn't good for his health. Most importantly, his Christian influence might be hurt when people find out that he hung out at this kind of party.

Option 3: Stay and use alcohol and/or drugs.

Positive: He will definitely get time with Sharon, and his friends will accept him as one of them.

Negative: This will be destructive to his health, and if the party is busted, David's in trouble. Regardless of whether he is caught or not, his Christian influence is shattered.

Bible:

1. 1 Corinthians 6: 19, 20 – "Or do you not know that your body is the temple of the Holy Spirit who is in you, whom you have from God, and you are not your own? For you were bought at a price; therefore glorify God in your body and in your spirit, which are God's."

PRACTICE DRILLS

2. Matthew 5: 16 – "Let your light so shine before men, that they may see your good works and glorify your Father in heaven."

3. 1 Peter 4: 3-5 – "For the time already past is sufficient for you to have carried out the desire of the Gentiles, having pursued a course of sensuality, lusts, drunkenness, carousing, drinking parties and abominable idolatries. In all this, they are surprised that you do not run with them into the same excesses of dissipation, and they malign you; but they will give account to Him who is ready to judge the living and the dead.."

4. 1 Corinthians 15: 33 – "Do not be deceived: 'Bad company corrupts good morals."

What should David do?

Option 3 is obviously not the right decision; there's no benefit brought to Christ and there's damage done in health and influence, much less the legal issues. With Option 2, there's always a possibility of being a good influence on others, but it comes with high risks. There will be problems to his health due to the smoke in the area. Also, while David may be attempting to be a good influence, someone may only see the situation as a Christian partying just like everyone else, which will damage his influence. There's only one good option – number 1. After putting all the options on the table and considering the positives and the negatives, David should simply leave the party. If Sharon is the type of girl that would stay and participate in the party then he should also begin looking for another young lady with the same goal that he has, the goal of Heaven.

GAME PLAN

Practice Drill #8 — Sexual Temptation

Pete can hardly believe Carly, the girl he is CRAZY about, has been showing so much interest in him lately. To his surprise, the more time they spend together, the more aggressive SHE is to become a more "physical" couple. Her advances are making it increasingly difficult for him to control himself. He doesn't want to give up the feeling her attention gives him, but he is worried things may get out of hand and go too far. What should he do?

Option 1: Give in to her advances.

Positive: He is taking action to secure her continual attention.

Negative: He is going against the morals and values that are an important part of his life.

Option 2: Never speak to or see her again.

Positive: He has removed the temptation she brings to his life.

Negative: Carly won't understand why Pete dropped off the face of the earth.

Option 3: Explain that he is really attracted to her, but her advances are causing him to feel uncomfortable.

Positive: He is being completely honest, and it may give them an opportunity to study the Bible's viewpoint on this subject together.

Negative: She may laugh at him, call him a "loser", dump him, and tell all their friends.

Bible:

1. Hebrews 13: 4 – "Marriage is to be held in honor among all, and the marriage bed is to be undefiled; for fornicators and adulterers God will judge."

2. 1 Thessalonian 4: 3,4 – "For this is the will of God, your sanctification; that is, that you abstain from sexual immorality; that each of you know how to possess his own vessel in sanctification and honor,"

PRACTICE DRILLS

3. 1 Timothy 4:12 – "Let no one look down on your youthfulness, but rather in speech, conduct, love, faith and purity, show yourself an example of those who believe."

4. 1 Peter 4: 3,4 – "or the time already past is sufficient for you to have carried out the desire of the Gentiles, having pursued a course of sensuality, lusts, drunkenness, carousing, drinking parties and abominable idolatries. In all this, they are surprised that you do not run with them into the same excesses of dissipation, and they malign you."

What Should Pete Do?

Even though he would miss the attention, as a Christian, Option 1 cannot ever be a possibility. While he would continue to receive the attention, his conscience would continually eat away at him as he would be convicted by his sin. Of the remaining two options, the last one seems to be the best approach to take initially. He might have a great impact on her if he talks with her; however, if she's not willing to listen, then Pete should take Option 2, and walk away. It's very easy to get pulled down, even when trying to help someone else up. Truth be told, Pete needs to seek the attention of someone else. If Carly is set on being sexually aggressive and has no boundaries herself, he would only be setting himself up for failure if he continued to hang around.

GAME PLAN

Practice Drill #9 — Pregnancy/Abortion

Kevin's best friend Tim has confided in him that his girlfriend is pregnant. Kevin is shocked to learn that Tim and his girlfriend Sarah let things go "that far", especially since Tim is a Christian. Sarah is considering having an abortion, terminating the baby's life, but Tim views his unborn child's life as sacred and doesn't think an abortion is such a great plan. Tim wants Kevin's advice, but Kevin is at a loss as to what to tell his friend. What should Kevin advise Tim to do?

Option 1: Let Sarah make the decision; after all, it is her body!

Positive: Tim is leaving the responsibility to Sarah, which will make him feel less pressure.

Negative: He is giving up complete control of his own child, which the Bible states he has a responsibility for.

Option 2: Post every nasty thing you can think about Sarah on all the social networking sites in order to "get back at her" for even thinking about making a decision without Tim's complete support.

Positive: Tim will feel better for "airing out" his feelings about his girlfriend.

Negative: It won't really accomplish much as far as a decision about the baby is concerned.

Option 3: Ask Sarah to meet with a counselor/minister to discuss their child, the future and what the Bible says on this subject.

Positive: They will be thinking through their decision as a couple, using God's Word to guide them.

Negative: One of them may leave with a different conclusion and decision than the other.

Bible:

1. Genesis 2:7 – "Then the Lord God formed man of dust from the ground, and breathed into his nostrils the breath of life; and man became a living being."

PRACTICE DRILLS

2. Proverbs 3: 5-7 – "Trust in the Lord with all your heart and do not lean on your own understanding. In all your ways acknowledge Him, and He will make your paths straight. Do not be wise in your own eyes; fear the Lord and turn away from evil."

3. Psalm 1:1-2 – "How blessed is the man who does not walk in the counsel of the wicked, nor stand in the path of sinners, nor sit in the seat of scoffers! But his delight is in the law of the Lord, and in His law he meditates day and night."

4. 1 John 1: 9 – "If we confess our sins, He is faithful and righteous to forgive us our sins and to cleanse us from all unrighteousness."

What Should Tim Do?

The solution to committing one sin is not to follow it up with another. There's no doubt that Tim and Sarah both crossed into lawlessness; Tim, as a Christian, must repent. Not only has he broken his covenant with God, he has brought public shame on the Church. When it comes to how he and Sarah can respond in an appropriate way to the pregnancy, Option 1 and Option 2 are simply not good responses. While Tim might want to lash out at Sarah, this will not accomplish anything positive. They need to sit down with someone who will guide them through this very difficult process, using the Word of God as the standard. In "going too far", they sinned; however, their lives aren't over. If handled according to the Bible, while their life plans are forever changed, they can be forgiven in the eyes of God.

GAME PLAN

Practice Drill #10 — Media

At one time, Frank was very careful about his media habits. He was very picky about the video games he played, the movies and TV shows he watched, and the music he listened to. Recently though, there have been some really popular songs with catchy tunes that he thinks are cool.
He starts thinking that it won't really matter if he listens to these songs, which only have a small dose of inappropriate content. After all, he is just paying attention to the beat. Soon after, Frank starts playing video games he wouldn't have dared think about just a few months ago. He feels justified because in "video world", the situations and scenarios are pretend anyways. The next thing you know, he is being entertained by shows on television he previously wouldn't have dreamed of watching. He laughs at inappropriate content, and doesn't think twice about the immoral lifestyles the characters are living. Now that he is caught up in this new world of media, what should he do?

Option 1: Keep up his new media habits.

Positive: He keeps enjoying the things he likes.

Negative: He is digesting content that is not good for his Christian walk.

Option 2: Limit his media intake.

Positive: He is not influenced as much by TV, music, and video games.

Negative: He is still digesting more than he should.

Option 3: Completely cut out all of his new habits.

Positive: He is getting rid of a lot of sinful habits in his life and has more time to concentrate on things that are holy.

Negative: He will miss many things he enjoyed.

Bible:

1. 1 Thessalonians 4: 3-4 – "For this is the will of God, your sanctification; that is, that you abstain from sexual immorality; that each of you know how to possess his own vessel in sanctification and honor,"

PRACTICE DRILLS

2. Matthew 15: 17-19 – "Do you not understand that everything that goes into the mouth passes into the stomach, and is eliminated? But the things that proceed out of the mouth come from the heart, and those defile the man. For out of the heart come evil thoughts, murders, adulteries, fornications, thefts, false witness, slanders."

3. Matthew 22: 37 – "And He said to him, " ' YOU SHALL LOVE THE LORD YOUR GOD WITH ALL YOUR HEART, AND WITH ALL YOUR SOUL, AND WITH ALL YOUR MIND."

4. 1 Corinthians 6: 17-19 – "But the one who joins himself to the Lord is one spirit with Him. Flee immorality. Every other sin that a man commits is outside the body, but the immoral man sins against his own body. Or do you not know that your body is a temple of the Holy Spirit who is in you, whom you have from God, and that you are not your own?"

What Should Frank Do?

As a Christian teenager, Frank knows better. The problem is that he has slipped into a desensitized state where the immorality presented to him through the media doesn't impact him as much. It's sad, but Frank's not the only Christian this happens to. Option 1 is not a valid option in light of Scripture. According to the Bible, Christians are to flee from immorality. If he chooses Option 2, he won't be running away from it, he will be allowing it to be a part of his life. Frank needs to choose Option 3. In order for this to take place, Frank will have to change his way of thinking and change his actions (in other words – repent). He might have to completely drop all forms of media for a time, just to break the habits he's created. Most of all, his prayer life needs to intensify as does his time spent in reading and studying the Word of God.

ENDNOTES

CHAPTER 1

[1] U.S. Census Bureau. American Community Survey (www.factfinder.census.gov)

[2] "teenager." Online Etymology Dictionary. Douglas Harper, Historian. 21 Sep. 2010. <Dictionary.com http://dictionary.reference.com/browse/teenager>.

[3] Abbott, W.W., editor. The Papers of George Washington: Colonial Series, Volume 1 (University Press of Virginia: 1983) p.9

[4] Palladino, Grace. "They're Getting Older Younger." Introduction. *Teenagers an American History*. New York: Basic, 1996. Xiii-iv. Print.

[5] U.S. Census Bureau. American Community Survey (www.factfinder.census.gov)

[6] Daniel, Eleanor Ann., and John William Wade. *Foundations for Christian Education*. Joplin, MO: College, 1999. 180. Print.

[7] Ibid. p. 180.

[8] Ibid. p. 182.

[9] Wilcox, W. Bradford, and Elizabeth Marquardt, eds. *The State of Our Unions: Marriage in America 2009*. Rep. The National Marriage Project, Dec. 2009. Web. 21 Mar. 2011. <http://www.virginia.edu/marriageproject/pdfs/Union_11_25_09.pdf>.p. 77

ENDNOTES

[10] "Erikson's Psychosocial Stages | in Chapter 11: Personality | from Psychology: An Introduction by Russ Dewey." Psych Web by Russ Dewey. 2007. Web. 27 June 2011. <http://www.psywww.com/intropsych/ch11_personality/eriksons_psychosocial_stages.html>.

[11] Ibid. p.99

[12] García, Jose, and Tamara Draut. *The Plastic Safety Net: How Households Are Coping in a Fragile Economy*. Rep. 2009 ed. New York, NY: Demos, 2009.p.3. Print.

[13] "The Decline of Marriage and Rise of New Families." *Pew Research Center*. 18 Nov. 2010. Web. 24 Mar. 2011. <http://pewresearch.org/pubs/1802/decline-marriage-rise-new-families>.

[14] "Our Lives, Our Music", *Rolling Stone*, November 26, 1992, 50.

[15] Schultze Et Al., Quentin J. "The Sayings of Chairman Bob." *Dancing in the Dark*. Grand Rapids, MI: Wm. B. Eerdmans, 1990. 192. Print.

[16] *Spin*, October 2005, 108.

[17] Grigoriadis, Vanessa. "The Adventures of Super Boy." *Rolling Stones* 03 Mar. 2011: 52-58. Print.

CHAPTER 2

[1] James McNeil quoted in Horovitz, B. (2006, November 22). Six Strategies Marketers use to Make Kids Want Things Bad. *USA Today*, p. 1B. Retrieved March 2, 2008, from http://www.usatoday.com/money/advertising/2006-11-21-toy-strategies-usat_x.htm.

[2] James McNeal quoted in BuyBabies. (2006, December 9). *The Economist*.

[3] http://www.money-management-works.com/teen-spending.html

[4] http://www.money-management-works.com/teen-spending.html

[5] http://www.money-management-works.com/teen-spending.html

[6] Palladino, Grace. "The Advertising Age." *Teenagers an American History*. New York: Basic, 1996. 101. Print.

[7] West, Diana. "The Twist." *The Death of the Grown-up: How America's Arrested Development Is Bringing down Western Civilization*. New York: St. Martin's, 2007. 25. Print.

GAME PLAN

⁸ Promotion Circulars, Scrapbook No. 1, EE Collection, NMAH.

⁹ Palladino, Grace. "The Advertising Age." Ibid. 103-104. Print.

¹⁰ Hechinger, Grace and Fred M. *Teen-Age Tyranny*. New York: Fawcett Publications, 1963. 149.

¹¹ http://rockhall.com/story-of-rock/

¹² Palladino, Grace. "Great Balls of Fire." *Teenagers an American History*. New York: Basic, 1996. 121. Print.

¹³ Jackson, John A. *Big Beat Heat: Alan Freed and the Early Years of Rock & Roll*. New York: Schirmer, 1991. 3-5. Print.

¹⁴ "A Warning to the Music Business," *Variety* 197 (23 February 1955): 2

¹⁵ Gillett, Charlie. *The Sound of the City: The Rise of Rock and Roll*. New York: Pantheon Books, 1984. 20-21. Print.

¹⁶ Palladino, Grace. "Great Balls of Fire." *Teenagers an American History*. New York: Basic, 1996. 128-129. Print.

¹⁷ The Ed Sullivan Show, January 6, 1957.

¹⁸ Blackboard Jungle. Dir. Richard Brooks. By Richard Brooks. Perf. Glenn Ford, Anne Francis, and Sidney Poitier. Metro-Goldwyn-Mayer, 1955. Film.

¹⁹ Gilbert, James Burkhart. *A Cycle of Outrage: America's Reaction to the Juvenile Delinquent in the 1950s*. New York: Oxford UP, 1986. 68. Print.

CHAPTER 3

¹ *Coldplay's Chris Martin*, Rolling Stone, June 26, 2008, p. 55.

² *Beliefs: General Religious*. www.Barna.org. 2007.

³ *Most Adults Feel Accepted by God, But Lack a Biblical Worldview*. www.Barna.org. August 9, 2005.

⁴ Dunphy, John. "A Religion for a New Age." *The Humanist* Jan.-Feb. 1983: 23-26. Print.

⁵ Turek, Frank. "CrossExamined.org - Frank Turek | Christians Beware: Intellectual Predators at College." *CrossExamined.org - Frank Turek | Christian Youth*

Are Leaving the Church. Web. 25 May 2011. <http://crossexamined.org/articles-detail.asp?ID=81>.

[6] Berube, Michael. "Teaching Postmodern Fiction without Being Sure that the Genre Exists." *Chronicle of Higher Education*, May 19, 2000.

[7] Shortell, Timothy. "Religion & Morality: A Contradiction Explained." *Axis of Evil: Perforated Praeter Naturam*. Qualiatica Press, 2004. P. 106-116.

[8] "Three Days of Hope." *Pennsylvania Gazette*. January/February 1999.

[9] "Globalization and its Discontents," TIME Europe Web Exclusive, 30 January 2000.

[10] "Interview: Steven Weinberg." *PBS: Public Broadcasting Service*. Web. 25 May 2011. <http://www.pbs.org/faithandreason/transcript/wein-body.html>.

[11] Gross, Neil, and Solon Simmons. "How Religious Are America's College and University Professors?" *Sociology of Religion* 70.2 (2007): 101-29. Oxford University Press, 6 Feb. 2007. Web. 25 May 2011. <http://socrel.oxfordjournals.org/content/70/2/101.abstract>.

CHAPTER 4

[1] "Statistics | Facebook." *Welcome to Facebook - Log In, Sign Up or Learn More*. Web. 22 June 2011. <http://www.facebook.com/press/info.php?statistics>.

[2] Twenge, Jean M. *Generation Me: Why Today's Young Americans Are More Confident, Assertive, Entitled--and More Miserable than Ever before*. New York: Free, 2006. P. 1

[3] Ibid. p. 53.

[4] Ibid. p. 53.

[5] Ibid. p. 55.

[6] *It is very questionable*: Baumeister, Roy. "The Lowdown on High Self-esteem: Thinking You're Hot Stuff Isn't the Promised Cure-all." *Los Angeles Times*, January 25, 2005.

[7] Coffey, Laura T. "Plastic Surgery for Teens: A Good or Bad Move? - Parenting - TODAY.com." *TODAY.com: Matt Lauer, Meredith Vieira, Ann Curry, Al Roker, Natalie*

GAME PLAN

Morales - *TODAY Show Video, News, Recipes, Health, Pets*. 30 Mar. 2010. Web. 27 May 2011. <http://today.msnbc.msn.com/id/36101073/ns/today-parenting/t/can-plastic-surgery-be-good-teens/>.

[8] "Plastic Surgery For Teenagers Briefing Paper." *The American Society of Plastic Surgeons*. Web. 27 May 2011. <http://www.plasticsurgery.org/news-and-resources/briefing-papers/plastic-surgery-for-teenagers.html>.

[9] "CHARACTER COUNTS!: Programs: Ethics of American Youth Survey: Josephson Institute's Report Card." *Character Education Program: CHARACTER COUNTS! - Lesson Plans, Training, Resources*. 26 Oct. 2010. Web. 27 May 2011. <http://charactercounts.org/programs/reportcard/2010/installment01_report-card_bullying-youth-violence.html>.

[10] "Warning Signs That Your Child Is Being Bullied." *School Violence | School Bullying | School Safety*. Web. 22 June 2011. <http://www.nssc1.org/signs-your-child-is-being-bullied.html>.

[11] "One Quarter (27%) Of American Teens Use Facebook Continuously Throughout the Day | Ipsos." *Ipsos North America | Market Research*. 5 Jan. 2011. Web. 27 May 2011. <http://www.ipsos-na.com/news-polls/pressrelease.aspx?id=5095>.

[12] "CDC - Injury - Youth Suicide." *Centers for Disease Control and Prevention*. 15 Oct. 2009. Web. 27 May 2011. <http://www.cdc.gov/violenceprevention/pub/youth_suicide.html>.

[13] "Youth Suicide." *Centers for Disease Control and Prevention*. Web. 13 June 2011. <http://www.cdc.gov/ncipc/dvp/Suicide/youthsuicide.htm>.

[14] "CDC - Injury - Youth Suicide." *Centers for Disease Control and Prevention*. 15 Oct. 2009. Web. 27 May 2011.

[15] Twenge, Jean M. *Generation Me: Why Today's Young Americans Are More Confident, Assertive, Entitled--and More Miserable than Ever before*. New York: Free, 2006. P. 109.

CHAPTER 5

[1] *Roe v. Wade*, 410 U.S. 113 (1973).

[2] "Fetal Development -- From Conception to Birth." *National Right to Life*. Web. 22 June 2011. <http://www.nrlc.org/abortion/facts/fetaldevelopment.html>.

ENDNOTES

³ Patten, Bradley M., and Bruce M. Carlson. *Patten's Foundations of Embryology.* 5th ed. New York: McGraw-Hill Book, 1988. p. 128-129. Print.

⁴ Report, Subcommittee on Separation of Powers to Senate Judiciary Committee S-158, 97th Congress, 1st Session 1981.

⁵ Kittel, Gerhard, Gerhard Friedrich, and Geoffrey William. Bromiley. *Theological Dictionary of the New Testament.* Grand Rapids, MI: W.B. Eerdmans, 1985. 759-60. Print.

⁶ http://www.nrlc.org/Factsheets/FS03_AbortionInTheUS.pdf

⁷ Jones RK, Finer LB and Singh S, *Characteristics of U.S. Abortion Patients*, 2008, New York: Guttmacher Institute, 2010.

⁸ *The Basics: A Compilation of Recent and Noteworthy Information on the Abortion Issue.* National Right to Life, May 2006. Web. 22 June 2011. <http://www.nrlc.org/>

⁹ Harrub, Brad. "Interview: Abby Johnson." *Think* February 2010: 10-12. Print.

CHAPTER 6

¹ Saad, Lydia. "Four Moral Issues Sharply Divide Americans." *Gallup.Com - Daily News, Polls, Public Opinion on Government, Politics, Economics, Management.* 26 May 2010. Web. 02 Feb. 2011. <http://www.gallup.com/poll/137357/four-moral-issues-sharply-divide-americans.aspx>.

² *Bowers v. Hardwick*, 478 U.S. 186 (1986)

³ Bell, Alan P., and Martin S. Weinberg. *Homosexualities: a Study of Diversity among Men and Women.* New York: Simon and Schuster, 1978. 303.

⁴ Kirk, Marshall, and Hunter Madsen. *After the Ball: How America Will Conquer Its Fear and Hatred of Gays in the '90s.* New York, NY: Doubleday, 1989. Print.

⁵ Ibid., xxvii.

⁶ http://voterguide.sos.ca.gov/past/2008/general/text-proposed-laws/text-of-proposed-laws.pdf#prop8

⁷ Moore, Maloy. "Tracking the Money: Final Numbers." *Los Angeles Times.* Los Angeles Times, 03 Feb. 2009. Web. 10 Feb. 2011. <http://www.latimes.com/news/local/la-moneymap,0,2198220.htmlstory>.

⁸ Kirk and Madsen, *After the Ball*, 146.

⁹ http://www.glsen.org/cgi-bin/iowa/all/library/record/2342.html?state=what

¹⁰http://www.nonamecallingweek.org/binarydata/NoNameCalling_ATTACH-MENTS/file/87-1.pdf

¹¹ Haan, Linda De, and Stern Nijland. *King & King*. Berkeley, CA: Tricycle, 2000. Print.

¹² Garden, Nancy, and Sharon Wooding. *Molly's Family*. New York: Farrar Straus Giroux, 2004. Print.

¹³ Tompkins, Crystal, and Lindsey Evans. *Oh, the Things Mommies Do! What Could Be Better than Having Two?* [S.l.]: Crystal Tompkins, 2009. Print.

¹⁴ Caplan, David. "Clay Aiken: No More Secrets." *People* 6 Oct. 2008: 72-78. Web. <http://www.people.com/people/archive/article/0,,20230468,00.html>.

¹⁵ LeVay, Simon (1991), "A Difference in Hypothalamic Structure Between Heterosexual and Homosexual Men," *Science*, 253:1034-1037, August 30.

¹⁶ Byrd, A. Dean, Shirley E. Cox, and Jeffrey W. Robinson (2001), "Homosexuality: The Innate – Immutability Argument Finds No Basis in Science," *The Salt Lake Tribune*, [Online] URL: http://www.sltrib.com/2001/may/05272001/commenta/100523.htm.

¹⁷ Bailey, Michael J., and Richard C. Pillard (1991), "A Genetic Study of Male Sexual Orientation," *Archives of General Psychiatry*, 48:1089-1096, December.

¹⁸ Bailey, Michael J. and D.S. Benishay (1993), "Familial Aggregation of the Female Sexual Orientation," *American Journal of Psychiatry*, 150[2]:272-277.

¹⁹ Hamer, Dean H., Stella Hu, Victoria L. Magnuson, Nan Hu, Angela M. L. Pattatucci (1993), "A Linkage Between DNA Markers on the X Chromosome and Male Sexual Orientation," *Science*, 261:321-327, July 16.

²⁰ Sorba, Ryan. "The 'gay Gene' Hoax." *WorldNetDaily*. 3 June 2010. Web. 13 June 2011. <http://www.wnd.com/index.php?pageId=161549>.

CHAPTER 7

¹ Hesketh, Ph.D., Therese, Li Lu, M.D., and Zhu Wei Xing, M.P.H. "The Effect of China's One-Child Family Policy after 25 Years." *The New England Journal of Medicine* 353 (2005): 1171-1176. *The New England Journal of Medicine*. Massachusetts Medical Society, 15 Sept. 2005. Web. 16 Mar. 2011. <http://www.nejm.org/doi/

ENDNOTES

full/10.1056/NEJMhpr051833>.

[2] Baculinao, Eric. "NBC: China Begins to Face Sex-ratio Imbalance - World News - Msnbc.com." *Breaking News, Weather, Business, Health, Entertainment, Sports, Politics, Travel, Science, Technology, Local, US & World News - Msnbc.com.* 14 Sept. 2004. Web. 16 Mar. 2011. <http://www.msnbc.msn.com/id/5953508/ns/world_news/>.

[3] Wallerstein, Judith S., Julia Lewis, and Sandra Blakeslee. Introduction. *The Unexpected Legacy of Divorce: a 25 Year Landmark Study.* New York: Hyperion, 2000. Xxiii. Print.

[4] Baskerville, Stephen. "Divorce as Revolution." *Salisbury Review* 21.4 (2003): 30-32. Print.

[5] Wilcox, W. Bradford, and Elizabeth Marquardt, eds. *The State of Our Unions: Marriage in America 2009.* Rep. The National Marriage Project, Dec. 2009. Web. 21 Mar. 2011. <http://www.virginia.edu/marriageproject/pdfs/Union_11_25_09.pdf>.p. 64

[6] Ibid. p. 68

[7] Ibid. p. 83-84

[8] Ibid. p. 85

[9] Bachman, Jerald G., and Patrick M. O'Malley. *Monitoring the Future.* By Lloyd D. Johnston. 2009 ed. Ann Arbor: Institute for Social Research, The University of Michigan, 2010. 174. Print.

[10] Ibid. p. 199

[11] *The State of Our Unions: Marriage in America 2009.* p. 111-113

[12] "Integrity." Def. 1. *Merriam-Webster, Inc.* Web. 25 Mar. 2011. <http://www.merriam-webster.com/thesaurus/integrity?show=0&t=1301100714>.

[13] *Josephson Institute's 2010 Report Card on the Ethics of American Youth.* 28 Mr. 2011. <http://charactercounts.org/programs/reportcard/2010/installment02_report-card_honesty-integrity.html>.

[14] Ibid.

[15] Golden, Paul. "THREE IN 10 AMERICANS ADMIT TO FINANCIAL DECEPTION WITH PARTNERS." *Www.nefe.org.* National Endowment for Financial Education,

GAME PLAN

14 Jan. 2011. Web. 28 Mar. 2011. <http://www.nefe.org/NEFENews/PressRoom/PressRelease/ADMITTINGTOFINANCIALDECEPTIONS/tabid/967/Default.aspx>.

[16] *Josephson Institute's 2010 Report Card on the Ethics of American Youth.* 28 Mr. 2011. <http://charactercounts.org/programs/reportcard/2010/installment02_report-card_honesty-integrity.html>.

CHAPTER 8

[1] Rideout, M.A., Victoria J., Ulla G. Foehr, Ph.D., and Donald F. Roberts, Ph.D. "GENERATION M2: Media in the Lives of 8- to 18-Year-Olds." *Www.kff.org*. The Henry J. Kaiser Family Foundation, 20 Jan. 2010. Web. 31 Mar. 2011. <http://www.kff.org/entmedia/upload/8010.pdf>.

[2] Ibid, p. 18-19

[3] Ibid, p. 28-29

[4] Ibid, p. 20-24

[5] Ibid, p. 15-17

[6] Ibid, p. 25-27

[7] "Habitat for Profanity: Broadcast TV's Sharp Increase in Foul Language." *Www.parentstv.org*. Parents Television Council, 2010. Web. 4 Apr. 2011. <http://www.parentstv.org/PTC/publications/reports/2010ProfanityStudy/study.pdf>.

[8] Ibid

[9] KunKel, Ph.D., Dale, Keren Eyal, Ph.D., Keli Finnerty, Erica Biely, and Edward Donnerstein, Ph.D. *Sex on TV 4*. Rep. The Kaiser Family Foundation, Nov. 2005. Web. 4 Apr. 2011. <http://www.kff.org/entmedia/upload/Sex-on-TV-4-Full-Report.pdf>.

[10] Beresin, M.D., Eugene V. "The Impact of Media Violence on Children and Adolescents: Opportunities for Clinical Interventions." *Www.aacap.org*. The American Academy of Child and Adolescent Psychiatry, 2010. Web. 4 Apr. 2011. <http://www.aacap.org/cs/root/developmentor/the_impact_of_media_violence_on_children_and_adolescents_opportunities_for_clinical_interventions>.

[11] *How Teens Use Media: A Nielsen Report on the Myths and Realities of Teen Media Trends*. Rep. The Nielsen Company, 2009. Web. 5 Apr. 2011. <http://blog.nielsen.com/nielsenwire/reports/nielsen_howteensusemedia_june09.pdf>.

ENDNOTES

[12] Kaufman, Gil. "Lady Gaga's 'Born This Way' Is Fastest-Selling Single In ITunes History." *Www.mtv.com*. MTV, 18 Feb. 2011. Web. 5 Apr. 2011. <http://www.mtv.com/news/articles/1658317/lady-gaga-born-this-way-itunes.jhtml>.

[13] Gaga, Lady. "Born This Way." *Lady Gaga*. Lady Gaga. Interscope Records, 2011. MP3.

[14] Ibid

[15] Eells, Josh. "Queen of Pain." *Rolling Stones* 14 Apr. 2011: 40+. Print.

[16] Rihanna. "S&M." *Loud*. Rihanna. The Island Def Jam Music Group, 2010. MP3.

[17] Sherman, Barry L., and Joseph K. Dominick. "Violence and Sex in Music Videos: TV and Rock'n'Roll." *Journal of Communication* 36.1 (1986): 79-93. Print.

[18] Anderson, Craig A., Nicholas L. Carnagey, and Janie Eubanks. "Exposure to Violent Media: The Effects of Songs with Violent Lyrics on Aggressive Thoughts and Feelings." *Journal of Personality and Social Psychology* 84.5 (2003): 960-71. Print.

[19] Rideout et.al., Ibid. p. 3

[20] *Is Social Networking Changing Childhood?* Rep. Common Sense Media, 2009. Web. 6 Apr. 2011. <http://www.commonsensemedia.org/teen-social-media>.

[21] *How Teens Use Media: A Nielsen Report on the Myths and Realities of Teen Media Trends*. Rep. The Nielsen Company, 2009. Web. 5 Apr. 2011. <http://blog.nielsen.com/nielsenwire/reports/nielsen_howteensusemedia_june09.pdf>.

[22] Rideout, M.A., et. al. Ibid, p. 20-24

[23] *The "New" Tube: A Content Analysis of YouTube - the Most Popular Online Video Destination*. Rep. Parents Television Council, 17 Dec. 2008. Web. 7 Apr. 2011. <http://www.parentstv.org/PTC/publications/reports/YouTube/NewTube.pdf>.

[24] "Pornography Statistics." *Family Safe Media - Parental Control Tools Including TV Guardian, Time Management, Filtered Internet, Telemarketing Blocks and More*. Web. 07 Apr. 2011. <http://familysafemedia.com/pornography_statistics.html>.

[25] Huesmann, L. Rowell, Jessica Moise-Titus, Cheryl-Lynn Podolski, and Leonard D. Eron. "Longitudinal Relations between Children's Exposure to TV Violence and Their Aggressive and Violent Behavior in Young Adulthood: 1977–1992." *Developmental Psychology* 39.2 (2003): 201-21. *Www.apa.org*. American Psychological Association, 2003. Web. 7 Apr. 2011. <http://www.apa.org/pubs/journals/releases/dev-392201.pdf>.

[26] Ibid. p.210.

CHAPTER 9

[1] Perry, Nick. "More Modest Clothing, Please, Girl Asks Nordstrom." *Seattletimes.com*. The Seattle Times Company, 21 May 2004. Web. 10 May 2011. <http://seattletimes.nwsource.com/html/localnews/2001934910_fashion21e.html>.

[2] Delgado, Ray. "Retailer Goes from 'Wong' Wrong to Thong / 2nd Controversy in 2 Months - SFGate." *Featured Articles From The SFGate*. San Francisco Chronicle, 22 May 2002. Web. 16 May 2011. <http://articles.sfgate.com/2002-05-22/news/17545398_1_abercrombie-fitch-thongs-abercrombie-spokesman>.

[3] Cox, Robert. "Now Playing in New Rochelle, "Book, Interrupted"! | Talk of the Sound." *Talk of the Sound | News for New Rochelle*. 08 Dec. 2008. Web. 16 May 2011. <http://www.newrochelletalk.com/?q=node/288>.

[4] Opelka, Mike. "Padded, Push-Up Bikini Tops for 8-Year-Old Girls? Again Abercrombie & Fitch Sexualizes Children." *The Blaze*. 27 Mar. 2011. Web. 16 May 2011. <http://www.theblaze.com/stories/padded-push-up-bikini-tops-for-8yr-old-girls-again-abercrombie-fitch-sexualizes-children/>.

[5] "Mother Claims To Inject 8-Year-Old With Botox, Perform Monthly 'Virgin Waxes'" *Breaking News and Opinion on The Huffington Post*. 24 Mar. 2011. Web. 16 May 2011. <http://www.huffingtonpost.com/2011/03/24/8-year-old-botox_n_839946.html>.

[6] Riechert, Tom. "History of Sex in Advertising." *Dr. Tom Reichert's Sexinadvertising.com*. Web. 17 May 2011. <http://sexinadvertising.com/History/index.php>.

[7] "Policy Statement - Sexuality, Contraception, and the Media." *American Academy of Pediatrics* 126.3 (2010): 576-82. *Pediatrics*. The American Academy of Pediatrics, 30 Aug. 2010. Web. 18 May 2011. <http://pediatrics.aappublications.org/content/126/3/576.full.pdf+html>.

[8] Rideout, M.A., Victoria J., Ulla G. Foehr, Ph.D., and Donald F. Roberts, Ph.D. "GENERATION M2: Media in the Lives of 8- to 18-Year-Olds." *Www.kff.org*. The Henry J. Kaiser Family Foundation, 20 Jan. 2010. Web. 31 Mar. 2011. P. 26. <http://www.kff.org/entmedia/upload/8010.pdf>.

[9] "Sex and Relationships in the Media." *Media Awareness Network | Réseau éducation Médias*. Web. 18 May 2011. <http://www.media-awareness.ca/english/issues/stereotyping/women_and_girls/women_sex.cfm>.

[10] "Policy Statement - Sexuality, Contraception, and the Media." *American Academy of Pediatrics* 126.3 (2010): 576-82. *Pediatrics*. The American Academy of

ENDNOTES

Pediatrics, 30 Aug. 2010. Web. 18 May 2011. <http://pediatrics.aappublications.org/content/126/3/576.full.pdf+html>.

[11] CDC. *Youth Risk Behavior Surveillance—United States*, 2009. [pdf 3.5M] MMWR 2010;59(SS-5):1–142.

[12] *Sex and Tech: Results From a Survey of Teens and Young Adults*. Rep. The National Campaign to Prevent Teen and Unplanned Pregnancy, 2008. Web. 19 May 2011. <http://www.thenationalcampaign.org/sextech/PDF/SexTech_Summary.pdf>.

[13] Sessums, Kevin. "Miley Cyrus 'I Know Who I Am Now' | Parade.com." *PARADE Magazine, Celebrity News, Entertainment News, Health, Fitness, Food, Recipes, Games | Parade.com*. 21 Mar. 2010. Web. 19 May 2011. <http://www.parade.com/celebrity/2010/03/miley-cyrus.html>.

CHAPTER 10

[1] *Habitat for Profanity: Broadcast TV's Sharp Increase in Foul Language.* Parents Television Council, 2010. http://www.parentstv.org/PTC/publications/reports/2010ProfanityStudy/study.pdf

[2] Smith, David R. "The Source for Youth Ministry - TheSource4YM.com." *Tons of FREE Resources for Youth Ministry*. 28 Feb. 2008. Web. 31 May 2011. <http://www.thesource4ym.com/youthculturewindow/article.aspx?ID=23>.

[3] Cohen, Jackie. "Oh, @#$%, Half Of Facebookers' Walls Have Profanity." *All Facebook - The Unofficial Facebook Blog - Facebook News, Facebook Marketing, Facebook Business, and More!* Mediabistro.com, 23 May 2011. Web. 31 May 2011. <http://www.allfacebook.com/oh-half-of-facebookers-walls-have-profanity-2011-05>.

[4] "SHGTUS -- Who Are the Tomb Guards?" Society of the Honor Guard - Tomb of the Unknown Soldier. Web. 23 June 2011. <http://www.tombguard.org/creed.html>.

[5] "The Unknown Soldiers - The Tomb Sentinals." Home Of Heroes Home Page. Web. 23 June 2011. <http://www.homeofheroes.com/gravesites/unknowns/0_unknowns_sentinels.html>.

APPENDIX

INTERVIEW WITH ABBY JOHNSON, PRINTED IN THE FEBRUARY 2010 ISSUE OF THINK MAGAZINE, PUBLISHED BY FOCUS PRESS, INC.

On September 26, 2009, Abby Johnson held an ultrasound probe as she watched a baby in the womb recoil from a suction cannula while a doctor performed an abortion. That horrific scene caused Abby to leave Planned Parenthood. She is now working for a pro-life organization called Coalition for Life.

Focus Press: Please share with our readers some of your background and how you became involved in the abortion controversy.

Abby Johnson: I was a student at Texas A&M and went to a volunteer opportunity fair that they had every semester on campus. There was a woman there who was talking about planned parenthood. I really didn't know anything about Planned Parenthood. I didn't grow up in a community with Planned Parenthood. She began talking about Planned Parenthood and the services they provided. She did talk about abortion a little bit, but she told us that the primary volunteer duties were to escort women into the clinic whenever they were there for their abortion procedures. I told her that I grew up in a pro-life household. She told me she understood that, but the reason it was so important for women to have this choice was because if it wasn't available then women would be having all of these illegal abortions and dying at this incredible rate. And I just thought this was terrible, so I thought to myself, "This is something I could get behind and it makes sense to me." So I started volunteering.

I was a volunteer for about two years. I then became their campus intern—still a volunteer position—but I became the liaison between Planned Parenthood and Texas A&M. I did that for a year, and right before I graduated with my undergraduate degree from A&M, they asked me if I wanted to become an employee—a paid employee—of Planned Parenthood.

APPENDIX

I didn't have any other job prospects coming up, so I said sure. I knew I wanted to get my master's degree and they said they would work with me on that. So I went ahead and started working there. I worked there through the time when I got my graduate degree and just kept getting promoted and eventually ended up running that particular health center.

FP: So, you actually grew up in a "pro-life" family environment?

AJ: Yes, absolutely!

FP: Wow. So what do you think it was that helped you make that break and say: "I'm going to volunteer for Planned Parenthood?" Was there a certain phrase or hook she used, or something that she was offering that made it appealing?

AJ: Well, I think it was just the idea that if legalized abortion is not available and if these clinics are not available, then we are basically sending women to these slaughter-houses. And therefore women would be dying at this incredible rate. And for me—I'm a very compassionate person—to hear that was too much. To hear somebody say, "Women are going to be dying if this is not a legal option for women" was new. I'd never really thought about it in that way.

FP: Even though the statistics don't bear out their scare tactic. So, in a weird, twisted kind of way you viewed yourself as "pro-life" but for older life, so to speak?

AJ: Right. Really that is the way they want to frame the argument. They don't ever think about the unborn life, and that is intentional. They don't want to think about the baby. They don't want the clinic workers to think about the baby. They don't want the women coming in for the abortions to think about the baby. They only want the women to think about themselves. And they only want the clinic workers to think about the woman sitting in front of them. And that's very intentional.

FP: Obviously there is a single event that changed your perspective on life. Can you share what took place and how it changed you?

GAME PLAN APPENDIX

AJ: There were a couple of things. One was how the business model had been changing within the facility. They had really gone from a family planning and prevention model to abortion model. They went to, "Abortion is the most lucrative. It's how we make the most money. We're not making any money with the economy, so we see abortion as an opportunity to really up our income and up our revenue. So we need to get in as many women as possible to have these abortions." So that was very troubling.

FP: Wow, that's incredible to hear.

AJ: And so that was kind of the first thing. When I questioned that, it was really my fall from grace. That was when my supervisor told me abortion needed to be my number one priority. That I really didn't need to worry about family planning and that I needed to get my head in the game for abortion. That's when I told her abortion would never be my priority, and that family planning would always be my priority. That's when things started to snowball for me.

On September 26 (2009), that's when I actually saw an ultrasound-guided abortion procedure. Ultrasound-guided abortions are very uncommon. They are particularly uncommon in large abortion facilities like Planned Parenthood. If we are talking about abortion in terms of safe procedures for the woman, ultrasound-guided procedures are the safest procedure. It is the best type of procedure for the woman. There's less risk of uterine perforation. These big places don't want to do it because it takes more time.

This particular physician who was coming down that day is a private practice abortion physician. He has his own practice out of town and he was coming in to do abortions as a visiting physician that day. In his practice he only does ultrasound-guided abortions. The patient was a little further along in her pregnancy—about 13 weeks—so the doctor decided that on this patient he was going to do an ultrasound-guided procedure. For that procedure he needed an extra person in the room to hold the ultrasound probe, and that was me.

So they called me into the room and told me they would need me to hold

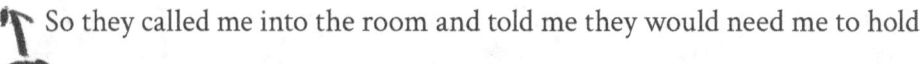

the ultrasound probe on her abdomen so that he could see the uterus during the procedure. That was to be my job during the procedure. So we had everything in place, and I saw on the screen a thirteen-week baby. You know at thirteen weeks—even at ten weeks—what you see on the ultrasound is a fully formed baby with arms and legs. Everything is fully formed. If you can get a good profile view, you can see all of this.

Well, this was a good profile view. I could see everything from head to foot. And then I saw the probe—called a cannula, that is hooked up to the suction machine—I saw that go into the woman's uterus. And then I saw it jab into the side of the baby. Then, in just a few seconds, I saw the baby begin to react to that jabbing. I saw the baby's arms and legs begin to move. The baby was trying to get away from the probe.

FP: Wow. I have to ask this because I'm sitting here trying to imagine it for myself: What were you going through internally at that point?

AJ: Well, I couldn't believe what I was looking at. I felt sick to my stomach. I realized what I was about to look at and I realized what I was about to see. And that's when they turned on the suction. A baby at that age has a perfectly formed backbone. The last thing I saw was the backbone going through the cannula on the ultrasound screen. I'll never forget what it looked like on the screen. You know how they say with a train wreck you don't want to watch but you can't stop looking at it? That's what it was like for me. I didn't want to look at it, but I couldn't stop looking at the screen. When I saw that baby moving, it was like he was waking up and then trying to get away from the cannula.

I immediately thought of all the women I had lied too. You get a lot of questions in the room. As a counselor in the room with women, they ask you questions before they go back for their abortion procedure. One of the things they ask you frequently is, "Is my baby going to feel this?" Every time I had told them no. Because I really didn't think the baby would feel it. Planned Parenthood had told me they wouldn't feel it, so I told them no. I immediately thought about all the women I had lied to. I was thinking to myself, "What if I had told them the truth? What if I had known the truth— would I still be here at this job? Would those women have chosen an abortion?" What kind of difference would it have made if we had all known the truth? Why are they trying to hide this?

FP: So obviously your beliefs have changed. What would you say today, here at the end of 2009, are your beliefs on this controversial topic?

AJ: I'm firmly pro-life. The other day I went out in front of an abortion clinic for the first time on an abortion day. It was a good feeling to be on the other side of the fence. But I have a very unique sense of what is going on inside that clinic and what those women are feeling, because I have sat there and looked in their faces.

FP: So what would you say? Let's say you have a 15-year-old or a 20-year-old or even a 30-year-old that is currently pregnant and not sure what to do? What would be your words of wisdom at this stage?

AJ: I've been asked that a lot. A lot of times women choose abortion out of convenience. In fact, most of the time they think that abortion is going to be a quick fix. They think an abortion is going to make their lives easier, and I **know** that is not the case. It is not a quick fix. It is not something you just do and it goes away. It will be with you for the rest of your life. If they are a young person or a person of any age and they don't have children—many women who choose abortion are in their younger years—that memory of the child they aborted comes back to them when they are holding their wanted children. People have asked me, "What would you have said differently to those women you were counseling with?" I would have said, "Your baby does have a heartbeat. No matter what you've been told, your baby does have a heartbeat, and your baby is going to feel what is happening to it during the abortion. Your baby is going to feel that pain. And, when the abortion is finished, somebody is going to have to go back and reassemble the baby that was in your uterus. And they are going to know if it was a boy or girl. This is very real. This is not just a mass of tissue. This is not just a glob of cells. This is a real baby in your uterus."

FP: What are the secrets in the abortion industry that many never hear about? Obviously you've touched on one that most people know that maybe we don't admit—and that is a lot of this is about money.

APPENDIX

AJ: Oh yeah.

FP: But what are some other things, having "been there and done that," that you can share?

AJ: It is so much about money. But also, anytime there are any complications they will do anything to keep that woman quiet, including paying her money to keep her quiet.

FP: Now when you say complications, you mean medical injury.

AJ: Yeah. They will pay her off to keep her quiet. Which is sad, because then we never know about those tragedies of abortion. There are so many times that women are injured from an abortion— they've had botched abortions— and instead of going to the media so that other women can hear their stories, they are paid off. They are required to sign a statement saying that they will not go public with that information. In some states, like Texas, there are laws where they will come and ask the woman if she wants to view the ultrasound. If she does choose to view her ultrasound, and let's say she's 10, 12 14, weeks pregnant, they will not show her the full profile of her baby. They may only show her...

FP: A leg.

AJ: The leg. If you are a layperson looking at the ultrasound, you don't know what that is. And they'll say, "That's it. See you can't see anything." Because they don't want to give her the truth. They call themselves pro-choice. But it's not really about giving women honest choices. There are just so many things they are not honest about. For instance, they never go over all of the risks about abortion when a woman comes in. They never talk about all of the options. They don't normally ask, "Have you considered your other options?"

FP: Have you ever seen someone coming back after an abortion procedure who is emotionally torn up?

GAME PLAN

AJ: Absolutely. Absolutely. The abortion industry's answer to that is that the person is weak or that they were emotionally unstable to begin with. They don't believe in post-abortion syndrome. They believe that for a normal person, you're going to do fine after the abortion. They really just dismiss women that have regrets after an abortion, and they just think something is wrong with them.

FP: We appreciate more than you know your willingness to talk. And we are so thankful you are speaking out for pro-life. I'll say this, I think there is a truth out there that is not getting out. I think if more women armed themselves with what you are revealing here, we would have less abortions going on than we have today.

COACH'S NOTES

COACH'S NOTES

COACH'S NOTES

COACH'S NOTES

COACH'S NOTES

COACH'S NOTES

COACH'S NOTES

COACH'S NOTES

COACH'S NOTES

www.ingramcontent.com/pod-product-compliance
Lightning Source LLC
Chambersburg PA
CBHW052018070526
44584CB00016B/1811